Power and response-ability
The human side of systems

Tom Graves
Tetradian Consulting

Published by
Tetradian Books
Unit 215, 9 St Johns Street
Colchester CO2 7NN, England

http://www.tetradianbooks.com

First published by Tom Graves April 2003 in electronic form only.
Revised edition published August 2008
ISBN 978-1-906681-14-2 (paperback)
ISBN 978-1-906681-15-9 (e-book)

Contents

Amongst others, the following people kindly provided comments and feedback on the early drafts of this book: Marcus Barber (Melbourne, Aus), Shawn Callahan (Anecdote, Aus), Holly Dinh (Melbourne, Aus), Nigel Green (CapGemini, GB), Elizabeth Hagiefremidis (Melbourne, Aus), David Holmes (DSTO, Aus), Liz Poraj-Wilczynska (Brockhampton, GB).

Please note that, to preserve commercial and personal confidentiality, the stories and examples have been adapted, combined and in part fictionalised from experiences in a variety of contexts, and do not and are not intended to represent any specific individual or organisation.

PRELUDE

A one-minute overview

1. The human side of systems – response-ability – is the management of power in the workplace.

2. In human terms, power is the ability to do work – more accurately work/play/relate/learn – as an expression of personal choice and personal response-ability.

3. A sense of meaning and purpose, a sense of self and of that which is greater than self, is important in creating personal power and productivity in the workplace.

4. The delusion that power can be taken from others through bullying and dominance (power-over) or offloading of responsibility and blame (power-under) reduces the availability of functional power in the workplace.

5. Transactions are always either win/win or lose/lose. Win/lose (zero-sum) is actually an illusory form of lose/lose.

6. These issues repeat at and between every level, from 'I' to 'We' to 'Us' to 'Them'.

7. Anything which supports power and purpose in an organisation's members, and in an organisation's transactions, will improve the organisation's bottom-line – whatever that bottom-line may be.

8. Anything which reduces power-over and power-under in transactions will improve the organisation's bottom-line.

9. Doing nothing about these issues impacts increasingly on the organisation's bottom-line - eventually leading to the death of the organisation.

10. Tools and techniques to assess, audit and address these issues are described here, and elsewhere in other sources.

11. You have the power to choose what to do next.

PREFACE

This book is a bit different from the others in the Tetradian Enterprise Architecture series – it's more of an extended essay than a workbook as such – so a bit of background might be useful before we start.

In essence, it describes the principles behind the tetradian concept: enhanced effectiveness via integration of four distinct dimensions – the *assets* of the enterprise – and power as *'the ability to do work'*, through which the aims of the enterprise can be achieved. The original (2001) version of the book predates by some years my current work on frameworks for whole-of-enterprise architecture, and draws on the research that I'd been doing for a decade or more before that, on what might be called 'enterprise psychology'.

Common themes throughout this work were around development of judgement and awareness, and of appropriate decision-making and action at all levels – from individual, to direct interpersonal, to the group and organisation, to an entire economy seen as 'enterprise'. Whatever the context – from learning new skills in the workplace, to issues of bullying at work and in the home, to enhancing engagement, effectiveness and excellence in any sense – it was clear that the core issues in each case were about personal power and personal responsibility.

Hence, as you'll see, the *Response-ability Manifesto* in this book. The text then expands on each of the statements in the 'manifesto', with an emphasis on how they apply in the business context.

I'll admit that some of what I wrote here is closer to a polemic than a measured academic thesis. There are no formal footnotes, and very few referenced sources: but these days, it's almost easier to look them up on the net and follow the cross-trails than to traipse through a morass of impenetrable citations. What I aimed for instead was to give some sense of the *feel* of how these issues work out in practice: as I said in one of the early chapters, most of the common – and supposedly 'proven' – notions of power in the workplace are so close to perfectly wrong in practice that it's amazing any work gets done at all…

For this book-format edition I've cleaned up the text somewhat, but it's essentially the same as in the original version. To update it fully, I would need to add many more references to complexity-science, and frameworks such as Cynefin – but these are already described in other books in the series, such as *Real Enterprise Architecture: beyond IT to the whole enterprise*. The basic theme on power has also been further developed in *SEMPER and SCORE: enhancing enterprise effectiveness*: the SEMPER whole-of-enterprise diagnostic uses the same scale, from actively-dysfunctional (power-against) to wholeness-responsibility (power-within and power-with), as a metric of 'ability to do work' in the various facets of the enterprise.

So the aim for this book is that it adds background and depth to the others, without duplicating the content. And the existing text does that, without needing much change: it stands well enough on its own. In line with the whole Tetradian series, its purpose is to present a much broader view of enterprise-architecture, as the architecture of an enterprise *as a whole*: if it succeeds in that, it will have played its part. I hope you find it useful, anyway.

Tom Graves
Colchester, England
July 2008

RESPONSE-ABILITY: A MANIFESTO

Systems

1. People are powerful. People make things happen, people make things work.

2. For convenience, we tend to partition work into systems – collections of related work-processes.

3. Every system is part of a larger system, all the way up to 'the everything'. Working on just one system at a time, it's easy to lose sight of the other parts that make up the larger system – or even of the system we're working with.

4. Within every system, every problem – no matter how complex, no matter how technical – can be resolved if there is commitment, drive, motivation. This power arises only from people: the human side of systems – 'response-ability' – is what makes everything work.

5. Many, if not most, of the methods used to control people, in order to control a system, actively reduce the availability of this human power. The result is systems – and hence work-practices – that are often ineffective, unreliable, inelegant and inappropriate.

6. By understanding, and respecting, the human side of systems, far more of that human power is released in support of the system and the shared purpose.

7. In many contexts, the human side of systems is the only one which really matters.

Economy and the 'bottom line'

8. The ways in which we work, and share the proceeds of that work with others, combine into what is loosely called 'the economy'.

9. The word 'economy' literally means 'the management of the household'. Hence the *real* economy encompasses far more than mere money: its concerns include the management of every aspect of the ways in which we interact with others, whether they involve money or not.

10. The economy exists on every scale, from individual one-on-one transactions, to the mass-markets of multi-national corporations.

11. Because money-management is so easy to quantify – whereas people-management isn't – it's all too easy to mistake the money-side of the economy for the whole economy, and that everything else can be ignored. It isn't, and we can't.

12. Balancing the budget for a huge corporation, or even a household, may not be easy, but it's the easiest part of the overall economy to manage. Managing people is *hard*.

13. One of the reasons why managing people is hard is that people don't respond well to being treated as objects, or as subjects of someone else's whims. Rule-books that forget to treat people as people deserve to be ignored.

14. The real bottom-line isn't just the bit where the finance-figures supposedly balance out, but where the *whole* of the economy balances out: all of our relations with *all* of our stakeholders.

Stakeholders and corporate culture

15. Stakeholders are people who have a stake in our work: our colleagues, customers, suppliers, shareholders, banks, unions, regulatory bodies, government and the wider community.

16. Ultimately, *everyone* is a stakeholder in our work, because what we do may, or does, affect everyone. For practical reasons, it may be easiest to regard as stakeholders only those people that are immediately associated with our work: but we need to remember that, at times, they may indeed include everyone.

17. Every organisation is a compound entity, a literal 'corporation' created from the interactions of its stakeholders. 'I' interweaves with 'We', with 'Us', and with 'Them' too.

18. At each level, the organisation – this compound entity – has its own persona, its own voice, made up of the choices of each stakeholder, and each cluster of stakeholders, in relationship with each other.

19. Another name for this persona or voice is 'corporate culture'.

20. Despite being made up of individual choices – or evasions of choices – this compound persona can be surprisingly stable. If we're not aware of it, it can swamp our own personality – changing us into yet another frustrated robot within the mechanisms of the machine.

21. Despite the desires of corporate management, corporate culture cannot be controlled – certainly not through something as crass as a company rule-book, at any rate.

22. The culture can, however, be provided with a direction, a sense of purpose.

Purpose and quality

23. Purpose provides the basis for an organisation's existence: the motivation and meaning for 'Us', as an organized association of individuals. Without that sense of purpose, nothing that the organisation does is done on purpose.

24. An explicit statement of purpose is the key foundation-stone for a functional quality-management process, such as TQM and ISO 9000:2000.

25. Without a meaningful purpose-statement to anchor them, quality-initiatives will invariably fail and fade away.

26. A purpose-statement must be something which provides a reason and focus for work, and which is credible and meaningful for all stakeholders.

27. To be meaningful, a purpose-statement isn't something to be knocked up by corporate management over a weekend retreat: it needs to be discussed with every stakeholder, to ensure that the stated purpose matches well with their own.

28. Once understood and committed to by all, the purpose-statement acts as the reference-point for all of the organisation's economic activity. Purchases, sales, policies, procedures, choices for hiring and firing – anything which purports to fulfil the organisation's purpose should be checked for alignment with the purpose-statement.

Knowledge

29. All individuals and organisations create and acquire knowledge, unique to their industry, their market and their purpose.

30. Knowledge is more than mere information. It is built up from the content and context of information, and the *connections* created between items of information.

31. Knowledge is dependent on people. All knowledge is created by people, either directly, or indirectly with the assistance of some kind of information-technology.

32. For the most part, knowledge resides in people, and often only in people.

33. On its own, information is meaningless. The 'information-technology revolution' of the past few decades has vastly increased the amount of information available to us, but most of it is unusable – and will remain so without a systematic knowledge-technology to create meaningful connections.

34. Most automated 'knowledge-management' tools do little more than provide repositories for unlinked and often unlinkable information.

35. Knowledge technology depends as much, if not more, on an understanding of people as it does of machines.

36. Information with a potential or actual application is often termed 'intellectual property'.

37. The intellectual-property system has become so misused that it is now little more than a legal fiction held together by lawyers' bluff. Mistaken attitudes about ownership now place everyone's work at risk.

38. The real intellectual property – the *use* of information – resides primarily in people's memory. Remembering is often hard, but forgetting is even harder: what is remembered cannot simply be forgotten on a lawyer's demand.

39. Important connections may be made via the accumulation of small, often unidentifiable and unrepeatable, items of information. The process is known as 'intuition'. "Discoveries are beyond the reach of reason: the role of reason is to follow afterwards and build a general theoretical scheme."

40. Intuition is literally 'teaching from within'. It is the basis of all skill and creativity.

41. Organisations are ultimately dependent upon individual skill and creativity.

42. Few organisations do anything to foster that skill and creativity. Many claim to do so – "our people are our greatest asset!" – but most actually crush it through clumsy handling of the human side of systems.

Work-relationships

43. People are not assets: they cannot be owned.

44. Describing people as assets, or as 'human resources', is an insult. 'People Strategies' isn't much better. Either way, organisations usually get what they ask for. Surly, disaffected robots tend not to be very productive. Organisations which *do* bother to respect the human side of systems tend to be very productive indeed.

45. An organisation's 'greatest asset' is not 'our people', but its *relationships* with those people. If not treated with respect, 'our' knowledge, skill, inventiveness and creativity will just walk out the door and go work someplace else.

46. Relationship-management is nothing new: for example, most large corporations use automated 'customer relationship management' tools.

47. Functional relationship-management only happens when *all* stakeholders are treated as co-creators in the organisation's purpose, and are treated with the same respect currently accorded only to customers, shareholders and senior management.

Power and response-ability

48. An organisation's productive activity arises from individual, *personal* power.

49. Misunderstandings abound regarding the nature of that power, and how it can be created, fostered and maintained in support of an organisation's purpose.

50. In physics, the definition of power (or, more accurately, potential) is 'the ability to do work'.

51. In physics, work is defined as 'the rate at which energy is expended'.

52. These definitions are implied when organisations treat people as work-objects or 'human resources'. In effect, slavery is equated with power: productivity is invariably poor, as most energy is expended on work without focus or purpose.

53. Objects don't have choice; humans do. Any definition of 'power' in human terms needs to acknowledge that fact of choice.

54. People express their power of choice through response-ability – the ability to choose and act upon appropriate responses to varying contexts.

55. Objects can never do more than react to circumstances: "to every action there is an equal and opposite reaction".

56. If treated as objects, people can never be more than reactive. When power and response-ability are fully acknowledged, people can also be *proactive* – planning for and acting upon future circumstances and future choices.

57. Organisations can prevent 'their' people from being proactive and productive, simply by treating people as objects. Most still do – with unfortunate results for all concerned. This can be avoided by working *with* – rather than against – the human side of systems.

Human forms of power

58. Any definition of power in human terms must include and express human choices and human needs.

59. In human terms, power is 'the ability to do work, as an expression of personal choice, personal response-ability and personal purpose'.

60. In human terms, work remains 'the rate at which energy is expended', as in physics. However, 'work' is anything – any process or purpose – upon which human energy is expended. To calm a fractious client, to reclaim composure from failure, or to hold true to a purpose, are 'work' just as much as are to dig a ditch or to solve a technical problem.

61. In human terms, there can be no clear distinction between 'work', 'play' or 'learn'. Each depends upon the other: they are different and necessary facets of the same human power.

62. In human terms, power is thus more accurately 'the ability to work / play / learn...' rather than 'the ability to do work...'.

63. The interwovenness of work / play / learn is demonstrated every day in every schoolyard – yet poorly understood in most organisations.

64. At any given time there will be a bias towards either 'working', 'playing' or 'learning', but over time all three must be in balance for any of them to occur consistently and productively.

Power in the work-environment

65. In organisations, 'work', 'play' and 'learn' map closely to purpose fulfilment, relationship management and knowledge technology. In any given aspect of the organisation's activity there will be a bias towards one or other of these areas, but all three must be in balance for activity to take place consistently and productively.

66. Attempts to exclude any part of the work/play/learn triad from any domain – "people come here to work, not play!" – will reduce the available power and purpose within that domain, and within other domains.

67. The common attitude that "work is what I do to pay for my play" leads to poor success and poor satisfaction in *all* domains.

68. A transitory balance of the work/play/learn triad may occur spontaneously, in individuals, groups and whole organisations, creating a brief burst of enthusiasm, creativity and productivity. Well-known examples exist in every industry: most, however, return to their normal torpor after mere few months, weeks or days.

69. Individuals and organisations that intentionally manage their balance of work/play/learn in each domain, and that work with rather than against the human side of systems, can sustain such 'phenomenal' activity indefinitely. Examples exist everywhere: however, most are, by intention, quiet achievers, and few are known outside their industry.

70. There are no hidden secrets to such success. All that is required for success is acknowledgement and respect of the human side of systems: respect of the fact that people are people.

Sources of power

71. People are powerful – if we allow them to be powerful.

72. *We* are powerful – if we allow ourselves to be powerful.

73. The *only* source of human power and response-ability is from within ourselves (power-from-within). This power cannot be given to us: we alone empower ourselves. This power cannot be taken from us: yet it can easily be stifled and suppressed, by others or by ourselves.

74. All work – work/play/learn – requires us to face the personal challenge and personal effort of that work. By assisting each other (power-with) to face that challenge, we can help each other to create and release personal power and response-ability for the chosen work.

Mistakes about power

75. People, being human, make mistakes about power. Organisations and the wider society, being made up of people, tend collectively to make the same mistakes – though often on a larger scale.

76. The idea that 'power is the ability to *avoid* work' is a common misunderstanding: this is almost exactly what power is not. Without work/play/learn to be done, there is no need for power. Many who claim that they want to 'be powerful' do not in fact want to do work: instead, they want to not *feel* power*less* – which is not the same thing at all.

77. Fear of powerlessness, or fear of challenge and effort, leads to a desire to attempt to 'export' those fears to others – trying to force those others to face such fears on our behalf.

78. An attempt at such export may take the form of trying to prop oneself up by putting others down (power-over). Common examples include intimidation, bullying, denigration and domination.

79. An attempt at such export may take the form of offloading response-ability to others without their involvement or consent (power-under). Common examples include rumour-mongering, misinformation, playing victim and, especially, the artificial manufacture of fear and blame.

80. All forms of power-over and power-under reduce the *overall* available power. Most energy is absorbed either in promoting or responding to the abuse – leaving very little for actual work.

Power-addictions, winners and losers

81. Despite the overall loss of power, both power-over and power-under tend to create the illusion that power has been co-opted from others. As a result, power-over and power-under can be highly addictive.

82. So common is this addiction that, for many people, exported power-over and power-under *is* 'power' – the only power they know or understand.

83. The resultant knock-on effect of this one mistake can cripple individuals, work-teams, divisions, organisations, industries and entire societies. In such situations, there are no winners: *everyone* loses.

84. In each transaction, there are only two choices: create power with each other, in a win/win; or attempt to export fears about power to others, in a lose/lose. The simplistic concept of win/lose (zero-sum) is actually an illusory form of lose/lose: this year's 'winner' is next year's loser.

85. Competition, for example, may be either win/win or lose/lose. Competition *with* others (playing to learn) is win/win; competition *against* others (playing to win) requires there to be losers in each transaction, and hence is invariably lose/lose in the long run.

Scope of power-issues

86. The same issues, and the same mistakes, repeat at every level, within each 'I', between 'I' and 'Thou', between 'I' and 'We', 'We' and 'Us', 'Us' and 'Them'.

87. As a result of mistaken notions about power and response-ability, in individuals, organisations and the wider society, power-over and power-under are more common – sometimes far more common – than power-with and power-from-within.

88. In organisations, the result of such confusions is invariably detrimental to the bottom-line – whatever the bottom-line of the organisation may be. Hence none of this is soft-psychology: it impacts directly upon all business practice.

Conclusions and actions

89. Anything which supports personal power-from-within and personal response-ability within a organisation's members will improve that organisation's bottom-line.

90. Anything which supports power-with and purpose within an organisation's transactions will improve that organisation's bottom-line.

91. Anything which reduces power-over and power-under within an organisation's transactions will improve that organisation's bottom-line.

92. Anything which supports the balance between purpose-fulfilment, relationship-management and knowledge-technology – 'work', 'play' and 'learn' – within an organisation, and within the members of that organisation, will improve that organisation's bottom-line.

93. Tools and techniques exist to assess, audit and address these issues – the human side of systems. Some are described in detail here. Others may be found elsewhere. They work: if applied consistently and with care within an organisation, they *do* create significant improvements in that organisation's bottom-line.

94. Doing nothing about these issues also has significant – but destructive – effects on an organisation's bottom-line.

95. As always, the response-ability, and the choice, is yours.

INTRODUCTION

People are powerful. People make things happen; people make things work.

When people are powerful, work really *does* happen. The productivity soars, the inspiration flows, the care and the commitment are omnipresent. Whenever that kind of enthusiasm occurs within an enterprise, everyone *wants* to work there, and work as hard as they can, because work at last feels worthwhile. And that's true regardless of the organisation's type – commercial, government, NGO, non-profit, whatever – and of the organisation's size, from a giant multinational corporation or government department, all the way down to the local Rotary Club.

All too often, though, things *don't* happen that way – or at least, don't happen in the way we want. Without apparent warning, the excitement and enthusiasm fade away to nothing; the 'Monday blues' become prevalent again; and it's back to the usual bitching and backbiting, the joys of office politics...

All of this chaos arises because of confusions about power and purpose: a failure to understand what power is, how to gain it, how to use it, how to share it, how not to lose it. In fact, many of the common concepts of power – especially within business – are so close to perfectly wrong in a functional sense that it's amazing any work happens at all. The results can be seen in almost every organisation: frustration, inefficiency and ineffectiveness, loss of motivation and morale, lost opportunities and, for commercial organisations, lost profits. It hurts. It hurts *everyone*.

Yet it needn't be that way. Those seemingly 'random' bursts of creativity and productivity at work aren't random at all: and the circumstances under which they occur can be easily understood. So it *is* possible to create, *and maintain*, the kind of enthusiasm and commitment to work that makes everyone's eyes open wide. It *is* possible to create, *and maintain*, a commitment to quality that has little to do with paper and procedures, but arises directly from people themselves. It really *is* possible to create, *and maintain*, conditions in which everyone involved can find a true sense of satisfaction, even joy, in work and elsewhere – with impressive impacts on every aspect of the organisation's 'bottom line'. Not just 'business as usual': a lot *more* than 'business as usual'!

And yes, there is a catch, of course. You won't get these results from some quick-fix fad, some kind of 'fit and forget' system. You'll get them only by paying systematic and consistent attention to the *human side of systems*: human power, and its expression as 'response-ability'.

Response-ability is all about personal power and productivity in the workplace: what it is, what it isn't, why it's worth developing, how to develop it, and how to prevent it from being destroyed.

So it depends not only on a different understanding of power, and relationships between people and organisations, but also on a different understanding of the nature of business itself, as a dynamic balance between three distinct themes: knowledge technology, relationship management and purpose fulfilment. And it requires continuous attention to quality – not just of products or services, but every aspect of the *human* quality of business, upon which the quality of products and services will ultimately depend.

Although this human side of systems deals with so-called 'soft' issues, its effects, and the results of measures taken, can be assessed, audited, addressed in the kind of 'hard' numbers that managers and other analysts need. And though its processes can at times be challenging, for everyone, the end-results *are* worthwhile, for everyone: I can promise you that.

So who should read this? It's aimed mainly at managers, consultants, union organisers and others who work with people in the workplace. Don't let that put you off, though, because it'll be relevant to anyone who wants to know more about their own power and response-ability, so as to get more of a sense of satisfaction and achievement from any aspect of their life. That'd be just about everyone, I'd guess? Let's see, anyway.

UNDERSTANDING EMPOWERMENT

Defining power

For our organisations to be effective, we need everyone involved to be as productive as they can. And that productivity, in turn, depends on the availability of power, in a human sense. So a clear understanding of power – what it is, and (often more important) what it isn't – is essential, to provide the foundation for functional responsibility at work.

But what *is* power, anyway? In some management texts, we'll see that power is linked with 'soft' concepts such as empowerment, commitment, motivation, quality – words which somehow seem to have about as much meaning as a wet fish, and about as easy to grasp. In other texts, power seems to be equated with control – whatever that might be, because it's evident no-one actually has it, no matter what they might try to pretend. And in common usage, too, 'power' is hopelessly ambiguous: power over self, power over others, a powerful leader, a powerful car, a powerful telescope, a powerful strike, a powerful blow – almost anything might be powerful. Or not. So power is, um... er... *power*, right?

In short, the usual concepts of power are a muddled mess. To get anywhere, we need to start again, with definitions that actually *mean* something. The simplest and safest place to start looking for concrete, objective meanings is in the sciences: and in physics, 'power' has a clear, straightforward, unambiguous definition:

Power is the rate at which work is done.

The physics definition for 'potential' is perhaps more relevant for the human context:

Potential is the ability to do work.

And 'work' too has a straightforward definition in physics:

Work is the rate at which energy is expended.

More accurately, it's the rate at which energy is changed from one form to another – a point that will become more relevant later. But that's about as far as physics will take us: 'energy' is essentially

3

defined as energy, which isn't very helpful. And in most sciences there's intentionally no concept of *purpose*, which does, however, have meaning in the human domain: the kinds of work on which energy is expended, and why that work is done, usually matter a great deal in business!

So where do we go next with this? To understand power at work, it's obvious we need to include the human dimension. So the first shift is that 'power' in human terms is essentially a description of *potential*, rather than the strict physics sense of power as the expression of that potential. Hence, in human terms, we could start with the definition:

Power is the ability to do work.

But if we try to use that definition without any other rider, we run into trouble straight away, because in effect we define slavery *as* power – not a good idea! And whilst objects and machines don't have choice, humans do: it's one of the things that makes us human. So at the least, we need to add the human dimension of choice, and the human need for a sense of meaning and purpose:

Power is the ability to do work, as an expression of personal choice, personal responsibility and personal purpose.

Here the definition of 'work' remains the same, as "the rate at which energy is expended". But it changes radically in sense, because 'energy' has many different meanings in a human context. So 'work' includes anything on which human energy is expended: digging a ditch is work, and likewise solving a technical problem – but so is managing a household or a corporation, or calming an angry client, or planning a future strategy. All of these, and many others, are 'work' – and in many cases we can *measure* the energy expended on that work, if only in nutritional terms.

So far, so good: in human terms – as in business – 'work' can be anything on which people choose to expend energy in a purpose-ful way, and 'power' is the ability to do that work.

But there's another essential human characteristic that needs to be added to that definition, though it's the source of many difficulties in business and elsewhere: it's that in human terms, there's no real distinction between 'work', 'play' and 'learn'. They're three differ-ent yet inextricably interdependent aspects of the same human energy: we learn, to extend our knowledge and ability; we practice those abilities through play, either on our own or with

4

others; we apply the results of that practice through work, on our own, and with others; which leads, in turn, and in time, to new learning, for ourselves, or shared with others.

This interwovenness of work, play and learn can be seen every day, in every schoolyard. Each depends on the other, and unless all of them are present – as in that dynamic balance of work, play and learn that can be seen in the schoolyard – *none* of them can happen. Trying to separate them, or partition them into separate domains, leads to endless problems and pointless inefficiencies.

And yet that kind of separation is exactly what most businesses, and even most people, would try to enforce. "You come here to work, not play!" is a common cry in business; employees learn to accept that "work is what I do to pay for my play", and settle down to doing the minimum work they can get away with: few people seem to realise there might be an important connection here... Those few organisations that *do* recognise the connection, and do intentionally integrate 'play' and 'learn' in the work of the organisation, tend to be very successful indeed.

So in human terms, we end up with a definition of 'power' that goes as follows:

> **Power is the ability to work/play/learn, as an expression of personal choice, personal responsibility and personal purpose.**

It's a definition that works: it can be applied directly in business and elsewhere, with concrete, measurable results.

But what about all those other colloquial meanings of 'power'? This doesn't say anything about getting power, or keeping power: how do we gain power, for example, or take it back from those who try to take it from us? What about power as control? What about – heaven forfend! – "power comes out of the barrel of a gun"? Where do those things fit within that definition?

They don't. That's the whole point: they don't.

Those other apparent meanings of 'power' arise from a series of delusions that have nothing to do with power itself. And until we recognise that they *are* delusions, we're going to get nowhere – which is what so often happens at present. So before we can go any further, we need to look at these delusory forms of 'power' – and start to face them within others, and within ourselves.

Power and delusion

We have a workable definition of power in human terms: but where does that power come from? The short answer is: from within each one of us – and *only* from within us. It doesn't drift around for us to grab out of thin air: it's part *of* us, an expression of us as human beings.

For example, imagine you want to cook a meal. You've invited some friends round, you want everything to be the best for them. (In a commercial context, just scale this up a bit: imagine you're doing the catering and presentation for a public event.) There's work to do, of many different kinds: plan the meal, get the ingredients, make a schedule so everything comes together at the right moments, tidy the room, lay out the table... the list goes on and on. Each of these tasks needs different kinds of energy, which tend to be given different names: to get started at all, for example, needs a specific kind of power that's usually called 'motivation'. But for each of those tasks, the power, and the energy, comes from you. Nowhere else. That's why power in this human sense is referred to as 'power-from-within'.

> **Power-from-within is the ability to source and access human power from within the self.**

Doing everything ourselves can be hugely satisfying. But sometimes it's not as much fun as doing it with others; and there are many things which we can't do only on our own. Perhaps the task is too big (as it certainly would be if you were catering for a public event); perhaps you don't know what to do; perhaps you're simply too tired. Either way, we can ask others for help. So you might ask a friend to show you how to do Thai cooking, perhaps; you might just need a bit of 'moral support' – and a suitable glass of wine? – to help you find that all-important motivation with which to get started. The only source of power, in human terms, is from within; but we can *share* that power with others, or help each other find that required power. This sharing of common purpose – particularly when its aim is to help us find our own power-from-within – is sometimes described as 'power-with'.

> **Power-with is the ability to assist each other to generate and access power-from-within, and to share that power with others.**

Yet in this sharing of power, a crucial delusion can easily creep in. Our only source of energy to do work – any kind of work – is from within ourselves. Everything needs energy, effort: it takes effort even to learn something new. But to *find* that energy within ourselves is often challenging – physically, emotionally, mentally or whatever. Facing the challenge, we don't feel powerful at all: often exactly the opposite, though we may not be conscious of the fact – indeed, in many cases we may be careful to *not* be conscious of it. That feeling of powerlessness is not pleasant: *no-one* likes facing it. And for whatever reason – and there are many, many reasons – up comes the delusion: the idea that we can banish that feeling of powerlessness by 'exporting' it – and, usually, the problem too – to someone else.

It *seems* to be so easy: pass the buck, find a scapegoat, trap someone else into doing the job for us. "Power is the ability to *avoid* work", says the delusion. And it *looks* as though it works – which is why it's such a common delusion. But it actually doesn't work: it *never* does, though it sometimes needs a lot of careful thought and observation in order to be able to recognise that fact. All that the delusion does is reduce the overall amount of available power. For one individual, or one group, for a short while, it may perhaps seem to increase their own power; but overall, over time, over the entire system or entire group of people, the total amount of power is *always* less – which means that less work gets done.

The delusion always takes one of two forms, whose usual names are perhaps a bit too pejorative for use in this context. We could call these forms 'Type A' and 'Type B', of course; but for consistency with 'power-with' and 'power-from-within', they'd best be described as 'power-over' and power-under'.

> **Power-over is any attempt, in any form whatsoever, to create the illusion of empowering the self by disempowering any other.**

The 'Godfather' slogan "true power cannot be given: it must be *taken*" is an obvious example of power-over; likewise the old Maoist assertion that "power comes out of the barrel of a gun". If a manager uses her supposed 'superiority' to bully a subordinate, that's power-over; deliberately setting out to humiliate someone is power-over; excluding others from involvement in decisions that affect them is power-over; spreading rumours about others, or intentionally misleading others, is power-over; so is kicking at the cat because you're feeling down. The details vary enormously, and impacts may vary enormously, but it's all the same delusion: the idea that we can prop ourselves up by putting others down.

The aim of power-over is to create the illusion that all the power has been 'taken' from others. By contrast, power-under *does* need others to be powerful – but only so that that power can then be co-opted by manipulation, by 'exporting' responsibility in some way:

Power-under is any attempt to offload responsibility onto another without their express involvement and consent.

(For that matter, attempting to *take* responsibility *from* another without their involvement and consent can also be power-under: the crucial issue is the lack of consent rather than the direction in which the responsibility is transferred.) Blame; scapegoating; 'playing victim'; dumping responsibility for work onto others: they're all forms of power-under, all variants of the same delusion that "power is the ability to avoid work". Power-under can some-times be a lot more subtle and a lot more difficult to identify than power-over: but the damage can sometimes be much more serious, precisely because it's so difficult to detect.

Power-over and power-under are extremely common – so much so that for many people, that's what power *is*. Some people make these delusions into a way of life; but *everyone* falls into them from time to time. To a large extent our entire society is held together – or supposedly held together – by power-over and power-under, through threats, punishments, edicts, demands, cajoling, bullying in many different forms. The Machiavellian office-politics pro-moted and popularised in books such as *The 48 Laws of Power* essentially consists of nothing but power-over and power-under. And so on, and so on – there's an awful lot of it about...

The usual name for power-over is violence; the usual name for power-under is abuse; as you'll now perhaps recognise from those definitions above, both are *extremely* common. If you don't believe me in this, think about those definitions for a while, then take a look around you: take a good look at most advertising and marketing; take a good look at other people's behaviour, at work and elsewhere; for that matter, take a good look at some of your *own* behaviour, at work and elsewhere.

Ouch...

And none of it works – that's what's so sad, so pathetic. Yet so very, very common.

It's all a delusion. We can't 'take' power from others: whether we want it or not it just doesn't work that way. We can't offload every responsibility onto others: it just doesn't work that way. Scape-goats have an uncanny ability to return just when they're least expected. None of it works: it simply doesn't work.

Ouch...

Yet because it doesn't work, but at first does *look* as if it works, it's also highly addictive. Therein lie a lot of problems, for everyone...

The addiction is perhaps more obvious with power-over. For example, imagine I'm your manager, but I don't feel in control of anything, including you or your work. So, feeling somewhat powerless, I try to 'export' that feeling to you: I try to prop myself up by putting you down, telling you you're no good at your job. What happens?

Either you ignore me, and get on with your work anyway; or you believe me, and become unable to do your work. If you ignored me, have I actually propped myself up? If you took on my 'put-down', am I actually in any more control – is any more work actually done – than before? In both cases, the answer's 'No': I might perhaps gain a brief delusion that I'm more 'powerful', but the overall power, in a functional sense, is less, because you now either can't, or won't want to, share your power with me. But because there's less work being done, I'm still not feeling power-ful: so I do it again... and again... and again...

Indulging in power-under is just as futile, and just as addictive. To go back to the meal example, let's say you want a Thai theme, but you don't know how to cook that way: so you might try to trap a friend into doing it for you – rather than *with* you. You might trap that friend in any number of ways: nagging to create guilt, perhaps – "you promised you'd do it for me last week, *and* the week before" – or 'playing victim' – "I can't do it, you've got to do it for me" – or flattery – "you're so much better at this than I am". It's now their responsibility, too: if the meal doesn't taste right, it's all *their* fault, not yours. "Power is the ability to avoid work", supposedly: if they're doing everything for you, you're obviously more 'powerful' there.

But what happens? Are you *actually* more powerful at all, from doing this? In reality, "power is the ability to work/play/learn": but here you've done nothing; learnt nothing. The smug feeling of having 'got away with' doing nothing is soon replaced by a flat feeling of emptiness and impotence. And what about next time you want a Thai meal? Having intentionally and deliberately learnt nothing, you're now dependent on increasingly unwilling friends: so to trap them into doing it for you again, you have to find another power-under trick... and another... and another...

The *only* source of power, in human terms, is from within ourselves. We can choose to share that power with others. *Anything else that calls itself 'power' is a delusion*: and an addictive delusion at that. It's a delusion that invariably reduces the overall amount of power available to do the work that we choose. It's also a delusion that's extremely common everywhere – including inside every organisation.

So in case you're thinking that this discussion of power still seems a bit abstract or academic, try a small costing exercise. Take a look at the usual office politics; take a look at all those put-downs and blame-games that run rife through almost every organisation. Take a good look at the place you work, the people you work with, the interactions you have with others. And note this one fact: *every occurrence of power-over and power-under will invariably and inevitably reduce the overall ability to do work.*

Take just a handful of examples, and ask yourself: what is the cost of each of those examples, in lost productivity, lost efficiency, lost morale? (A hint: whatever cost you come up with at first will be a wild *under*estimate, because of the knock-on effect of attempted export and counter-export.) Work out a typical cost for each type of incident. Then multiply that average by the total number of incidents (and yes, there'll be a lot of them...) within each area of work. And then let that hidden cost work its way through the balance-sheet, all the way down to the corporate 'bottom line' – whatever that 'bottom line' might be. That's the *real* cost of failing to minimise power-over and power-under at work. That's the *real* cost of failing to understand the real nature of power.

Ouch...

Not quite so abstract now?

Failing to face these issues effectively hurts organisations *real* bad. Hurts *you* real bad, too.

Ouch...

Export and import

Yes, it really *is* that bad. But if the problem's that bad, what can we do about it? More to the point, is there anything we *can* do about it? It's at this stage that a sense of futility tends to creep in...

10

And that feeling of powerlessness is exactly what I'm on about. Notice how *you* respond to that feeling, because that'll show you, first-hand, exactly how the delusion works – and also what you can do about it. But first you have to notice what your response actually is: because most of the time, most of us go to quite a bit of effort to *not* notice it.

It usually goes through several stages – which happen to illustrate exactly the different forms of the delusion.

The first response – especially in business environments – is often some variant on the ever-popular theme of 'shoot the messenger': an active form of power-over to express what's technically known as 'denial'. You try to export your discomfort to me, as the 'messenger' who appears to be the cause of that discomfort. You don't like what I say: so you throw away this book, rage at me, say I'm a liar, demand to have me fired, whatever... And yes, I might well run away in fear and terror at your anger, so yes, you might think that you *have* exported the discomfort to me. But none of this changes the fact that what I've described really *is* fact: so where's the power to work with those facts? The facts are still sitting there, "large as life and twice as natural": but now no-one has any power to cope with them. Oops... Delusion #1...

Some people, as we know all too well, never manage to get past that stage. But the next stage, as the feeling of impotence drifts back once it's clear that nothing has really changed, is often to slump down into the passive form of power-under. You want to blame me, or everyone else; if you can get past that, you may want to blame the world at large for not being *fair*. You might blame *yourself*, exporting responsibility to yourself in the past; or pro-crastinate, exporting responsibility to yourself in the future. More likely, you'll want to pass the buck to someone else – *anyone* else – to make it their responsibility, their fault. You might well put a lot of effort into that last part – effort which, if you think about it, you could otherwise have used in finding a more useful solution. And although you might find someone else who's able to take on the responsibility, the chances are fairly low, because, as we've seen, *everyone's* likely to be stuck in this particular delusion. And again, none of this activity – or, more often, passivity – changes the fact that the facts are still sitting there, completely unchanged. Oops... Delusion #2...

Many people never get past that stage either, and remain per-petually stuck in trying to export 'the problem' to someone else.

But in business especially, where people pride themselves in their ability to take charge, there's often a third stage: the active form of power-under. Once we recognise that passing the buck doesn't work – because there's no-one to pass the buck *to* – we eventually come back to the old phrase "the buck stops here": and instead of trying to export the problem to everyone else, we try to *import* it from everyone else. We try to take control. Of everything. For everyone (since clearly they're not going to do it themselves). And of everyone (since clearly they're not going to do it themselves). Oops... Delusion #3...

Big delusion... perhaps the biggest delusion of all...

Like all forms of the delusion, it looks good at first – it *looks*, and usually *feels*, like 'the right thing to do'. But... no. Or rather, it depends on what our motives are – not the motives we'd probably like to *think* we have, but the real ones that we're likely to be very careful not to notice. Go back to the definition of power-under: notice that "the crucial issue is the lack of consent rather than the direction in which the responsibility is transferred". Did everyone *ask* us for our help, our 'protection'? Did everyone *ask* us take control of every aspect of their behaviour and their lives? For that matter, could we do it? Would we actually succeed? It's fairly obvious that the answer's going to be 'No'...

So what's *really* going on here? In almost every case, what's really going on is that we're using the apparent import as a cover-up for our own export – in other words trying to use 'being responsible about everyone else' in order to *avoid* being responsible for our *own* behaviour. Which is why it doesn't work: because ultimately the only person we can be responsible for is ourselves.

Others can be responsible about us, and to us – that's power-with, in fact – and we to them; but not *for* us, not *for* them. The difference is subtle, yet utterly crucial. *The only actions and behaviours we can be responsible for are our own*: everything else is either attempted export or attempted import, in order to avoid that responsibility. When two people try to take responsibility from each other so as to avoid facing their own, the result is called 'co-dependency'; when more than two people try to do this, the result is called, simply, a mess. We can't live others' lives for them: it's exactly as possible, and exactly as sensible, as trying to go to the toilet for them. Others can't live our lives for us: it's our responsibility, and no-one else's. We can't 'take' responsibility from others, any more than we can 'take' power from others: it just doesn't work.

So what *can* we do? Answer: go back to those original definitions about power. We *do* have the power-from-within to address every kind of problem – including this one. And with awareness of others, we *do* have the possibility of power-with, helping each other to face these delusions. In principle, and in practice, all that we need to do is watch our responses, watch for our reflex tendency to fall into one or other of the 'power' delusions – and then choose a different response.

That's all there is to it, in principle. But not so easy in practice, especially in the everyday chaos of work and other people: it's a mess out there – a *big* mess. If we're honest, it's probably a big mess 'in here' within ourselves too... But there is one bit of good news: if it's as bad as all that, even quite a small amount of effort can create a large improvement – so the effort *is* worthwhile!

Winners and losers

There are a few other issues we still need to face, though, before we can start to turn this round. One of them – perhaps the most important – is the concept of 'winners' versus 'losers'.

"Winners are grinners": *everyone* wants to be a winner – feeling powerful, feeling on top of the world. Conversely, *no-one* wants to be a loser – feeling down, feeling lost, feeling powerless... no-one wants to face that feeling of powerlessness. But wait a minute: we've seen this before, haven't we? Something about being so uncomfortable with the feeling of powerlessness that we 'have to' export it to others? Just how much is that going to affect the 'need' to be a winner? Oops...

Dead right: there's another delusion at work here – or rather, another way in which the same delusions about power get played out. And as usual, the delusion starts with a simple mistake, leading in turn to *big* problems we see all around us, every day.

The mistake is about the availability of power: where it comes from, where it goes, who has it, who doesn't have it, how to gain it, how to lose it. The common-sense view of human power is that it's a fixed quantity, much like many other resources. It's 'out there', somewhere – though no-one seems to know quite where. And it's apparently divided up like a pie, with each person some-how – again, no-one quite knows how – assigned their own share of power. Since the size of this pie is fixed, all power-transactions between people must re-divide the pie, with gains and losses always adding up to a 'zero-sum'. As one Marxist theorist put it, "it is in the nature of power that it is impossible for one to have more without others having less". No other choice, apparently.

This 'win/lose' view of power tells us that we can *only* be a winner – *the* winner – by making someone else lose. And we win *by* making others lose: we *need* them to lose, and know that they have lost, in order for us to able to win. Worse, in this perspective, there's also no link between personal effort and personal power: instead, if we want to be powerful – *feel* powerful – all we have to do is make someone else lose. So we don't need to make any effort to win: all we have to do is make sure that others lose. And when we make someone lose, we take their power – and export power-*less*ness to them in its place. That's the idea, anyway...

We've already seen what goes wrong when there's any attempt at export. Yet here, in win/lose, we have a structure which actually *requires* it. It doesn't take much to guess the result: power-over and power-under run rampant, and thought before action is conspicuous mostly by its absence. *Not* wise...

This 'pie-slice' view of power also tells us that if we're feeling powerless – feel we've somehow been 'oppressed', made a loser – that must surely mean someone else has purloined some of our share of power. Hence, not surprisingly, we want it back. But what if everyone else is feeling powerless and oppressed, too? Who's stolen all our power? There must be a hidden oppressor here – we need to find them and strike back! No-one seems to know what power really is, but we know when we *haven't* got it: and we'll fight *anyone* for it – to the death, if necessary!

This zero-sum view of power is so simple, so clear, so easy to understand – and seductively, dangerously, lethally wrong. It's the source of countless battles for 'market share' and 'mindshare', the source of countless wars, countless revolutions and, yes, countless oppressions – and ultimately it's completely wrong. Sure, there's *some* truth in it: but often only because others have fallen for the same mistake, too, and think that *they're* fighting for or protecting their own so-fragile share of power. Total chaos, anyone? Free gift of chaos with every simple mistake? Oops...

Business – and much else besides – can be a lot less troublesome, and a lot more profitable, once we can bring ourselves to understand and accept that this simplistic pie-slice view of power isn't just an unnecessary assumption, it's just plain wrong. Yet to many people in business, my Darwinian description above isn't wrong at all – that's the way that it really *is*. It's a tough world out there: it's 'survival of the fittest', dog-eat-dog, y'know?

Ever stopped to wonder why, though? Ever stopped to consider the possibility that all this pain and struggle and chaos might just be the result of one simple mistake?

The mistake is that power isn't 'out there' at all, as some kind of fixed resource that we have to fight others for. It's 'in here', arising from within us, as part of us – and the only ones we might need to fight, to gain it, is ourselves.

It's not even a fixed resource: it's always there, from within us, in any amount. Power is our *own* ability to do work, or play, or learn, as an expression of our own choice, our own purpose. And it's not others, but *we*, who apply limits to its availability from within us, for all manner of different reasons – some of which we've already seen, in the previous discussion on power.

It's true that it can be hard to find that power from within ourselves – mainly because it's so easy to shut it down. That's the real reason why power-over and power-under don't work: not only is energy wasted in setting up the attempted export, but most people shut down when they detect – even unconsciously – an attempted export, so the power is no longer there to 'take' anyway.

If this isn't obvious already, look at the productivity of slaves. Not very high at the best of times, is it? What happens when a workforce gets pushed too far by management? They shut down – they work-to-rule, or go on strike – so that there's *less* 'ability to do work' as a result of the bullying, not more. What happens if you push a prospective customer too far? They shut down – and you don't make the sale. What happens if you use power-under tricks with a prospective customer? Yes, you might make the sale this time, but they'll shut down automatically in future – they won't be a repeat-customer – and they'll probably warn off all their friends and colleagues, too.

In each interaction, we have only two choices, two possibilities of shared power: win/win, or lose/lose. Either everyone wins; or no-one wins. *Win/lose is actually an illusory form of lose/lose.*

> For that matter, so is 'lose/win' – a mistaken notion of power-with in which I assume that I can only help you win by making myself lose. Putting myself down to prop you up is merely the other side of the power-over delusion; whilst pretending to do so – a common sales ploy – is just another kind of power-under, and just as ineffectual in the long run.

The pie-slice view of power – zero-sum, win/lose, lose/win, with all the power being somewhere 'out there' – seems like common-sense: but like so much apparent 'common-sense', it's completely wrong. Every time you, or I, or anyone, plays power-over or power-under, *everyone* loses. There are no winners in win/lose: only losers. It may not look like it at first, but that really *is* what actually happens.

So that's our choice: win/win, or lose/lose. We can play power-over games and power-under games as much as we like: but whenever we do so, everyone loses – including ourselves. Or we can explore the possibilities for power-with, to help each other find the appropriate power-from-within, to do the work / play / learn that arises from our shared purpose – and with care, and awareness, *everyone* wins, every time.

If we want to win, we have to make sure that everyone else wins with us.

And it's our choice, and our responsibility, every time.

Rights and responsibilities

Responsibility is where and how we express our choice. But even here problems can arise, which we need to note before moving on to exploring power within the business arena. The delusion that "power is the ability to *avoid* work" means that accepting responsibility is often equated with powerlessness, a 'successful' export of responsibility to someone else. And the habits of power-under lead, all too often, to a situation in which responsibility is equated with blame – "*who* is responsible for this mess?" yells an irate administrator, for example – and in which anyone who's willing to take on the responsibility for tidying up some kind of chaos immediately gets blamed for everything else as well. This doesn't help in getting the work done... but both are very common, in all kinds of work-environments.

More subtle yet are the confusions that arise over rights and responsibilities – especially when people think in terms of 'rights *or* responsibilities'. The problem is that statements like the US Bill of Rights or the UN's 'Universal Declaration of Human Rights' give the impression that rights are automatic, inherent and so on: but in fact every 'right' is an assertion that responsibilities are to be placed *on others* to uphold that right on our behalf. And some of those assertions of 'right' can be very arbitrary indeed, such as the

16

supposed 'jus primae noctis' – 'right of first night' – claimed by some mediaeval warlords over any newly-married couple under their so-called 'protection'. The concept of rights can lead straight to the dishonesties of power-under, the offloading of responsibility onto others without their consent – as is particularly evident wherever an argument is phrased in terms of "I have rights, *you* have responsibilities!"

Interestingly, and perhaps most disturbingly for business, even the concept of ownership falls far too easily into this trap, because it's usually defined in terms of property-rights, rights of *possession*, without any definitions of matching responsibilities. "If I own it, it's my right to do what I like with it": in effect, ownership is defined as 'the right to exploit without reference to others, either in the present or elsewhen'.

> There's also an associated 'anti-ownership', an asserted 'right' to *avoid* the 'anti-property' that no-one wants, such as pollution, poor food, poor living conditions, poor health and poor life-expectancy. Poverty brings unwanted 'riches' of the unwanted, it seems.

This all seems at first to be straightforward common-sense: but as with the pie-slice view of power, it doesn't work. Possession is deemed to confer rights without responsibilities: so the matching responsibilities have to be imposed separately through another route, through the cumbersome chaos called 'the Law' – and even then some people spend their entire working lives trying to find loopholes that would give them the 'right' to evade those responsibilities. In other words, power-under again, just like the pie-slice view of power – but institutionalised on a society-wide scale.

As we'll see later, there are some specific problems about ownership 'rights' in relation to business. And there are also many arguments about 'workplace rights' and the like. But in practice, in trying to create a more functional approach to power in the workplace, the concept of 'rights' itself often tends to be more of a hindrance than a help. More to the point, it actually isn't necessary: assertions of rights often result in evasions of responsibility, but defined responsibilities automatically lead to, and implicitly define, concomitant rights.

In Britain at least, the simplest illustration of this is traffic law. Despite the common-sense concept of 'right of way', there's in fact no such right: technically, a 'right of way' is actually a *responsibility*, on a land-holder, to permit passage of people and (usually) vehicles along a defined route across the land-holder's property.

The law then specifies a series of rules and responsibilities, indicating who must give way to whom, and under what conditions. Each rule is accompanied by explicit reasons for the respective responsibilities. Finally, there's a 'none of the above' kind of rule which says that road users are responsible at all times to drive safely, regardless of what anyone else is doing, and regardless of what any of the other rules might say.

So no-one is assigned arbitrary 'rights' over others: *no-one* has an automatic, inalienable 'right of way' over everyone else. There's no such right as a 'right of way': yet as a result of a complete, clearly-defined set of interlocking responsibilities, in effect *everyone* has 'right of way' appropriate to their needs, and in relation to everyone else's needs.

Given the prevalence of power-over and power-under, the concept of rights all too easily leads to power-problems: but we can get exactly the same result as was intended by the concept of rights, by starting instead from responsibilities. And in doing so, we bypass most of the power-over and power-under: when we *know* that there's no such right as a 'right of way', there's not much point in fighting others for it...

The possessive rights-based concept of ownership all too easily creates a tangled mess of assertion and counter-assertion, blame and counter-blame; but we can start instead from responsibilities, and replace it with a concept of *stewardship* – an acknowledgement of responsibility rather than assertion of right. In functional terms, it comes out much the same, it even *looks* much the same: the difference is that it works, where 'rights' and 'possession' don't.

I'd perhaps better add – especially in a business context! – that there's nothing wrong with ownership as such. Stewardship works better as a concept because it enforces an awareness of power as 'the ability to do work', where possession invites a lapse back to an attitude that power is the ability to avoid work.

In the same way, the common habit of equating responsibility with acceptance of blame suggests that 'responsibility' itself needs a different name, too. In the functional form of responsibility, in this context, what we need to emphasise is its relationship to functional power, as opposed to the delusions of power-over and power-under. And we need to emphasise responsibility as the *expression* of that power and choice, both in a personal sense as power-from-within, and shared with others as power-with. We can do this by describing responsibility as 'response-ability':

Response-ability is the ability to choose and act upon appropriate responses to events, in relation to personal purpose and shared purpose.

Response-ability is the expression of power as the personal and shared 'ability to do work': so there's no point in trying to 'be powerful' unless there's work to do. Response-ability is the expression of personal response to changing circumstances: it's an ability varies from person to person, from moment to moment. And response-ability is also the expression of personal choice and personal purpose – which reminds us that the human need for *meaning* must be included within our concept of human power.

Motivation and meaning

Another key area of confusion is around what's often described as the spiritual dimension of work. The usual problem-area is the word 'spiritual' itself: many people seem to think it's somehow connected only with religion, and hence has no real role in business – other than perhaps keeping industrial chaplains on call, to help staff with problems at home. But in fact it's the other way round: religion, in whatever form, is simply a tool to assist spirituality – but so too is work itself, if the circumstances are right. The confusion is so severe and so prevalent that the term 'spiritual' needs an explicit definition for the work-context:

The spiritual dimension of work is the personal experience of meaning, purpose and belonging – a sense of self and of relationship with that which is greater than self, within and through the process of work itself.

Once again, I mean 'work' here in that wider sense earlier: a dynamic balance of the three facets of 'work', 'play' and 'learn'.

Spirituality is sometimes described as 'inner power' or 'inner strength' – which tells us that it's essentially the same as what we've earlier seen as 'power-from-within'. More accurately, it's the *source* for that inner power. Without it, the availability of power slowly fades down to a kind of maintenance level, where nothing much happens at all – and stays that way until there's a good reason to find the energy to rekindle the inner fires again. We don't have to look far for examples: think of the well-known effects of 'de-skilling' an area of work, or the devastation of work-force morale after repeated 'restructuring' and 'downsizing'.

The process of reclaiming and maintaining that inner power, and using it in productive work, is generally described as 'motivation'. But herein lies another common mistake: the idea that people are only motivated by external inducements or external forces, and that, as leaders and managers, we're responsible for providing that motivation for 'our' people. In reality, we don't 'motivate' others at all: people motivate *themselves* – and they're the only ones who can do it.

It's true that 'motivational' speakers and the like can certainly help at times: but if we push people too hard that way, it'll just feel like an attempt at power-over or power-under – which means that they'll shut down, and we're then worse off than where we started. Bringing in motivational speakers to 'rally the troops' also tends to reassert the illusion that the power is 'out there' rather than 'in here': hence although productivity may rise for a while, it soon slumps back – often leading to an addictive dependence on 'motivational' support just to keep going.

The key to successful motivation lies in understanding its relationship with the spiritual dimension. Personal power arises from a personal sense of meaning within work, or associated with that work; it arises from a sense of purpose, that the work fulfils some personal need, some personal thread or theme of life; it arises from a sense of self – especially a sense of self identified in and with work; and it arises from a sense of belonging to some purpose or process greater than the immediate limitations of self, a sense of belonging to and jointly expressing some shared common purpose. All of these things matter: ultimately, they're the source of our power, and the power we share with others.

As with the 'work/play/learn' triad, all of those facets of the spiritual dimension need to be in balance for that power to be fully available. This is as true for organisations as for individuals. So yes, people *can* do work that has no meaning to them; people *can* get by on clockwatching, on an attitude that "work is what I do to pay for my play"; people *can* function, after a fashion, with Machiavellian self-centredness and an obsession with "what's in it for *me*?". But productivity and creativity will invariably be poor – and such people usually bring others down with them as well.

If we look at what *does* get people going, it always has those same four elements: the work feels meaningful; there's a feeling that it aligns with a personal sense of purpose; there's a sense of personal identification with the work, and the quality of that work; and

20

there's a sense of membership and commitment not just to the group or organisation, but to the wider community as well.

It's a bit unfortunate that for most people the best-known context that fulfils all these conditions is war. It's one reason why so many organisations end up being run – even in peace-time – as if they were on a war-footing, stumbling from one crisis to another in order to create a sense of urgency and excitement. So it's important to remember that support for all the facets *can* be created and maintained in ordinary, everyday work – and with a lot less stress on all concerned. We'll be looking at this in detail later.

Part of our power, though, is that we can *create* meaning in order to do work that we otherwise wouldn't want or be able to do. Even the most interesting work has periods of drudgery and boredom; all of us have aspects of our work that we dislike, or that we'd rather not face. To do that work, we have to create power from somewhere: we motivate ourselves to do it. And we usually do so by linking the work with something else that *does* have meaning, that *does* connect with our own sense of purpose.

Many people go to work day after day, year after year, in mind-numbing, dangerous, dirty jobs, and keep going by connecting it with the idea that by doing so they're supporting the family they love. And they can fall apart completely on divorce or separation, or when the family leaves home – because the supposed 'reason' to work goes with them. These are described as spiritual issues: yet they have very real impact on people's ability to do their day-to-day work – in other words, their power, in a human sense.

The spiritual dimension also indicates that people need a sense of self – a clear sense of who they are, and of their own *personal* purpose in life – in order to be able to identify with and be committed to their work. This is another reason why the delusions of power-over and power-under cause so many problems in organisations: the aim of both delusions – especially power-over – is to crush the sense of self of the Other, to create the illusion that power has been 'taken'. For example, think of a typical 'shoot the messenger' scenario: after a full-on yelling-at, or worse, for the sin of being the bearer of bad news, the 'messenger' is likely to feel crushed, worthless – and possibly unable to work for quite a while... Many organisations still operate on the inane principle of "the beatings will continue until morale improves", thinking that this style of power-over is somehow 'motivating' – and then wonder why their workforce laugh at them, and come back with the old retort that "the morale will continue until the beatings improve!"

All too often, the common concept of motivation regards people as little more than mindless robots that need to be rewound from time to time. Instead, it's far more sensible to realise – and respect – that people *are* intelligent, and motivate themselves when we don't stop them from doing so. People do know when extra effort is needed – and often know this better than their so-called 'leaders'. "We knew times were hard", they said, "so we'd put our shoulders to the wheel, ready to push, ready to take the strain – and then the idiots took the wheel away!"

Time and again, the same old pie-slice mistake about power rears its head: but the reality is that we don't 'give' people power through motivation, any more than we can 'take' it through power-over or power-under. If we want to 'motivate' people to do work, we need to understand it not as 'giving' power to others, but as power-with, as a work-oriented support for their own spiritual process: and where they can find a sense of meaning and purpose in work, and both a sense of self and that which is greater than self within that work, *people motivate themselves* to find their own power-from-within.

Expressing empowerment

The same mistakes that we saw with motivation also often occur with the concept of empowerment. The errors all arise from the usual source, namely the pie-slice view of power. In that view, the manager or great leader 'empowers' her staff by magnanimously giving to them some of her own power, or power that she, in turn, has been given by others 'above' her. In return for this gift of empowerment, her staff must use that power in carrying out the work that she ordains. As a model of the empowerment process, it's clear, it's simple, it's easy to understand, it's just plain common-sense – and it's completely the wrong way round. Which is why things get into such a mess...

It's best to admit, right from the start, that much of that common notion of empowerment is – to use somewhat outdated slang – little more than an ego-trip for the supposed 'empowerers'. We all like the illusion that we're the ones who 'give' power to others. The reality, though, is that *we* don't empower others at all: *people empower themselves* – and may then choose to share *their* power with *us*. So our real task, if we want others to be empowered to work, or play, or learn, is simply to be aware enough to not *stop* them from being so. Most of the time, the main problem is not lack of power from 'above', or 'out there', but people meddling so much that the power *can't* arise from within as it otherwise would. Hence, most of the time, all we have to do to 'empower' people is to remind them that they are powerful already – and then get out of their way, to let them get on with the work as required.

That process of 'reminding others that they are powerful' is part of what I earlier described as power-with. How we do it, what we need to do – or not do – and what type of power we need to encourage them to find within themselves depends on the context and the requirements. It's often also highly individual, because something that excites one person may be entirely unappealing to another: one reason why an understanding of the *personal* nature of 'life-purpose' is so important to empowerment. It also depends on an understanding of the real nature of power, as something that arises *from* the individual rather than something that is 'given' *to* them. And it depends on an awareness of the expression of power as response-ability – the ability of individuals to choose and act upon *appropriate* responses to current conditions.

We'll be seeing many examples of this as we go along. In practice, the process of functional empowerment always includes the same elements as motivation: exploring ways in which the work – whatever it is – can be perceived by the individual as worthwhile and meaningful to them and to those they see as associated with them; as being aligned with their own desires, needs and aspirations; as being something with which they can identify, and express themselves; and in which they can gain a sense of belonging, and a sense of contributing to a greater whole.

Given the prevalence in society in general of delusions about power, one of the complications is to find a way of empowering that doesn't simply replicate the problems of power-over and power-under at a larger scale. For example, it's quite easy to create a sense of urgency – and thus motivation of a kind – by inventing a sense of risk or threat: for business, as I mentioned earlier, the obvious example is war.

It's also why many 'motivation' models emphasise an image of 'Us against Them'. For example, one luxury-car company has, as a key part of its 'mission', the statement "beat Benz!". The catch, as we'll see more later, is that it doesn't work, in the long run, or in the wider scale: if we *do* 'beat Benz', or whatever, the only group left to 'beat' is ourselves... leading to an implosion of infighting of a kind that's destroyed many an otherwise seemingly successful organisation. 'Us against Them' is just another form of the power-over delusion: the *only* way that individuals, or groups, or whole corporations, can 'win' is by creating forms of empowerment that ensure that *everyone* wins.

That's empowerment; that's power. And we now need to move this discussion out of the abstract, and into the practical world of business – starting with a review of the ways in which these power-issues repeat within and between every scale of endeavour, from 'I' to 'We' to 'Us' to 'Them'.

I AND WE AND US AND THEM

Spheres of influence

Each of us has our own power; each of us has our own persona, the 'mask' with which we face the world; and each of us has our own sphere of influence, our own direct area of response-ability. Often we want to extend that sphere, for a while at least – perhaps to do work that we cannot do alone, or to gain access to resources that we cannot reach on our own. To do this, we have to share: share power, and response-ability, with others. Expanding the scope at each stage, one person becomes a member of a team, a department, a company, a corporation; 'I' becomes 'We', becomes 'Us', in relation to 'Them'. And that triad of 'work / play / learn' becomes a tetrahedron, with 'relate' as the new dimension taking us beyond the purely personal realm.

Yet in the midst of that sharing of power, the same old issues, the same old mistakes, repeat themselves at every level. Individuals try to prop themselves up by putting others down; teams try to offload responsibility onto other teams; departments and companies try to 'win' by making others lose. It all seems so normal – especially as some resources really *are* 'zero-sum' – that it's hard to see that none of this in-fighting actually works. All it does is reduce the overall ability to do work, for *everyone*.

Much of the problem arises from an inability to be aware of a scope wider than the immediate sphere of influence – a problem often made worse by unnecessarily restrictive 'need to know' policies, with results that are best described by the phrase "never let the left hand know what the right or middle hands are doing". It's also easy to imagine that power-over and power-under do actually work, when the feedback from such 'games' between departments or companies may take weeks or months to return.

But perhaps a better way to understand these problems is to think of them as a failure to manage appropriately the *boundaries* of each sphere of influence: boundaries of space, of time, of response-ability and, especially, boundaries between self and others. When we join a team, it's easy to think that we *are* the team, that our ideas, actions and choices are the centre of the team's existence. If we don't do this, in fact, we may well feel instead that we *aren't* a member of the team at all, that we have no reason to be there, and hence no reason to work – the 'motivation' issue again.

Yet the same is true for *every* member of the team; and the same issues repeat at every level. The accounts department may think it's *the* centre of the company, the sole reason for the company's existence, around which everything else in the company revolves. This sets the stage for some massive misunderstandings...

Though we can see these misunderstandings at work in a business environment, their source actually goes back to early childhood – and specifically, to the development of awareness of the boundary between 'I' and 'not-I'.

Right at the beginning, our world consists entirely of 'I', in which we experience impressions and events that we can't really resolve into anything specific – a kind of world of 'is-ness'. There are impressions we like, and ones we don't – and about which we may make a great deal of noise! – but otherwise there's no real way to differentiate between them. Our sphere of influence – or at least awareness – seems to encompass everything that there is.

Over time, though, we develop an awareness that some of those impressions have definite links to 'I', so we set about exploring the immediate limits of that 'I': watch a baby playing with its feet, for example. By the time we get fully mobile, and develop a sense of volition, we reach a stage dreaded by every parent: the 'terrible twos', the time of tears and tantrums... and the time when delusions about power-over and power-under first become established.

At this stage of childhood, what's going on is that we now have a clear idea that there *is* such a thing as 'not-I': and we don't like it. At all. We haven't yet grasped that things exist independent of us: we *know* that 'I' is the centre of the world, around which everything revolves. We're just gaining control of our body; we should be able to control anything, everything, in the same way. When 'not-I' doesn't do what we want, our sphere of influence suddenly seems to shrinks into a small ball of frustrated anger.

So we try to take control of 'not-I' too – a parent, a toy, another child, whatever it might be. And we do so by treating 'not-I' either as an *object*, a 'thing' without volition or needs of its own; or as our *subject*, an entity which we believe we're entitled to use as we wish, because – to our perception – it exists only as a sort of semi-attached extension of ourself.

An object-based attitude is one in which the Other is regarded as an inanimate object entirely separate from self.

A subject-based attitude is one in which the Other is regarded as a subject which exists only as a subordinate extension of self.

Object-based attitudes tend to surface as attempts at power-over; subject-based attitudes tend to surface both as power-over and power-under, but especially the latter. As you can imagine, both these perspectives on reality can cause *big* problems – especially in a crowded kindergarten full of similarly self-centred toddlers!

It's only at a much later stage of development – around five to eight years old – that it finally sinks in that 'not-I' can be another person, just like us, with whom we need to negotiate when our spheres of influence and interest overlap. Even so, those childish object-based and subject-based attitudes are always there, still lurking in the background – and can pop back up again even in the most unexpected places, whenever we face some difficulty about overlapping spheres of influence.

When life is too frustrating, it's easy to fall back into an imaginary world in which we alone are the centre: falling into power-over, treating others as objects, as robots that exist only to do our bidding; or power-under, cajoling, bullying, nagging others into changing themselves to conform to our wishes. Or both, of course.

So once again, the same issues repeat at every level: it's not just individuals, but teams, departments, whole corporations that can fall into this trap. We see a lot of it in company rule-books and the like: "All members of staff shall...". Yet people don't respond well to being treated as objects, or as subjects of someone else's whims: which is why there's so much office-politics, and why the rule-books so often get ignored, even when they genuinely need to be followed. And it's also why sales-staff who think they 'own' their customers, or companies that think they 'own' some market-share, are often in for a nasty surprise. It's a real problem.

It's a bit embarrassing, too, to realise that many company hand-books and company policies echo the obsessive self-centredness of a two-year-old, trying to 'control' others without understanding that others are perfectly capable of controlling themselves in their own way...

27

But we don't solve the problem by pretending it doesn't exist. Instead, we aim to get the whole company to 'grow up' – in a metaphoric sense – by testing, checking, reviewing our individual and collective interactions with others. We learn to identify old habits of power-over and power-under at every level; and replace them with new habits of power-with – of *negotiation*, rather than 'control' – wherever our spheres of influence need to overlap those of others with whom we share our world and work.

Hidden voices

A key part of this negotiation depends on a recognition not only that each level – 'I', 'We', 'Us', and 'Them' as well – has its own sphere of influence, but also has its own persona, its own voice. 'Persona' is the Latin word for 'mask', but also translates literally as 'that through which I sound': as we'll see, both meanings are relevant here, in a business context.

In law, a formal organisation such as a company is considered to be a legal person in its own right, a compound entity or body comprised of, yet legally distinct from, the human bodies with which it's associated. Company law defines rights and responsibilities of such 'incorporations', though with some odd anomalies to regular law: for example, companies can have limited liability, where individuals can't; and companies can own other companies, whereas individuals – fortunately! – can't own other individuals.

Yet this idea of a compound entity is more than a convenient legal fiction: at the level of persona, it's entirely real. It's what we experience as 'corporate culture', for example. A compound persona such as a team or department or company – or, more visibly, a football crowd – is not just the sum of its human parts, nor (usually) the lowest common denominator of those parts. Instead, in a very literal sense, it has a life of its own – one that can swamp the personas, and lives, of those who make up that entity, simply because it *is* 'greater than self' relative to each individual.

Our persona is not 'I' as such, but more a mask of habits through which we feel safe in interacting with a world 'out there'. Those habits, in effect, also indicate what we're likely to do well and not do so well: which is why attempts to map those habits through 'personality testing' of some kind are common in business, especially in recruitment.

One of the best-known tools is the Myers-Briggs Type Indicator, or MBTI, derived from Jungian theory, which identifies sixteen distinct 'psychological types'. Other models, such as a nine-type model known as the Enneagram, are more useful in that they also map personality changes under varying levels of stress. Transactional Analysis, and the classical Chinese five-phase model used in Group Dynamics, are more useful still in that they map habits of *interaction* as well as static choices. Yet this mapping applies at more than the individual level: using statistical correlations, we can also use the same tools to build a fairly accurate picture of the persona of a larger group – the larger-scale habits and patterns of behaviour underlying corporate culture.

A crucial point is that much of the 'personality' is not fixed: it's just a habit. Good personality-mapping tools can identify habitual patterns of behaviour, our reflexive 'non-choices': but even though those habits may be reinforced strongly by body-type and background, they *are* just habits, and we *can* choose alternate actions and responses in any circumstance. That's our power; in a very literal sense, that's our response-ability.

Our habits are our reflex-response behaviours, of both body and mind, which we've built up either through consciously learning a skill – such as typing, or driving a car – or simply through the pressures and demands of our everyday life. These responses are fast – and hence often more productive, where they're appropriate – precisely *because* we don't have to think about them. But that's also why they cause us, and others, all manner of problems.

If we learn to create a gap for choice between event and response, wherever required, and practice what we've learnt within a safe environment – otherwise known as 'play' – we can greatly reduce those problems. In the process, we greatly increase our *overall* productivity, for ourselves and with others. The same applies on larger scales: as we become more aware of choice as individuals, we also create choice for 'We' – the persona in the direct interactions we have with others, such as in teams and work-groups – and for 'Us' – the persona in our indirect interactions, at the level of department, division, company and corporation.

Individual change can be hard, not least because there's a strong tendency to think that we *are* our habits, our usual ways of working with the world. Yet *'I' is not that which changes, 'I' is that which chooses*. Whoever we are, whatever we do, and however we do it, we still remain ourselves – and the same applies to organisations.

Yet cultural change, at the levels beyond the individual, is often harder still, because it's not just the habits of individuals that need to change, but habits of interaction *between* those individuals and groups that need to change, too.

Unsurprisingly, there can be a lot of resistance to such change, not least because it brings people to the discomforting realisation that their individual and collective habits *are* only habit, and not 'just the way things are'. For organisations, there also needs to be an awareness that people don't so much resist change as resist *being* changed – especially when changes seem only for the benefit of others, or for no-one at all. It should be no surprise that attempts to change corporate culture by 'edict from above' don't work: the resistance to enforced change is too great. Change only happens by *negotiation* with all involved – creating power-with so that *everyone* wins through the change.

There's a subtle but serious complication, though, to do with the nature of persona as 'mask'. It's an issue that seems little understood in business, and the most useful studies have actually been from improvisational theatre – though that's an excellent practice-ground for business-folk who need to think fast on their feet! The problem is that although the individual or collective persona-mask – whatever that persona might be – is 'only' a collection of habits, those habits do have a kind of life of their own: we have choices, but in effect so too does the mask.

This is most evident if the mask can be perceived in some way as partially separate and distinct from ourselves. In 'impro' theatre, it's been found that this applies particularly to the kind of half-mask which covers the eyes and upper face but leaves the lower face and mouth exposed – a good metaphor for many business roles... Such Masks can develop a kind of 'vocabulary' of their own, which tends to be expressed – often unconsciously – by each and every wearer of the Mask. So whenever we put on a meta-phoric Mask – such as, in business, by taking on a work-role, or joining a work-team or a company – we necessarily enter into negotiation with the respective Mask. If we're not aware that we *are* in that negotiation, our own choices can be swamped, because the Mask's vocabulary and voice will seem to be our own.

Whoever we are, we can find ourselves acting out the habits of the role-persona, the Mask 'through which I sound' – thinking that they're our own habits, our own choices. Most people in business will know all too well that feeling of being 'taken over' by a role, or by the demands of corporate unanimity: it's almost like 'being possessed' by the role, the group, the company. In large organisations especially, with strong peer-pressure and a strong corporate culture, this 'take-over' can happen very fast indeed, with measurable change in new employees in less than a day, in some cases. The persona of the organisation is so much 'greater than self' that there's little space left for any other kind of 'I'. If this happens to us, our own sense of self may well falter and fade, perhaps almost to nothing – and with it our 'ability to do work', because personal power and response-ability ultimately depend on clear awareness of our own 'I'.

It's a serious problem. And it's one that isn't helped by the fact that many organisations, by their structure and sheer size, tend to trap themselves into treating their staff as work-objects, or as mere subjects of the corporate will, or both – and thus, in the quest for some kind of control and unanimity, create systems that will inherently reduce the overall 'ability to do work' in the enterprise. The only way out of this trap is to be aware of a natural tendency of *all* groups towards object-based and subject-based attitudes about their individual members; and instead to design systems which support – rather than crush, smother or silence – individual power and individual response-ability.

Systems within systems

For convenience, and for other practical reasons, it's a common practice to partition work into 'systems' – collections of related work processes with defined inputs and outputs and, usually, defined activities. Having partitioned work in this way, it's then easy to fall into the trap of thinking that these systems, and the boundaries between them, are natural and inherent in 'the way things are' – rather than recognise the reality that, ultimately, all boundaries are entirely arbitrary.

In practice, many apparent boundaries exist not for functional reasons, but as ways to conceal structural or habitual power-over and power-under – especially the latter, as 'offloading of responsibility to another'. Think of that excuse of 'computer error': "we billed you for $10,000 instead of $100 because of a computer error" – what exactly *was* this mysterious computer error? Software? Hardware? Network? If – as is likely – it's nothing to do with the computer as such, but a keying mistake, whose responsibility *is* it?

The operator? The supervisor? The training department? The software developers, or testers, for not including real-world limit-checks on data-entry? The keyboard makers, for designing and building a keypad on which an operator could add a couple of extra zeroes by mistake? In a blame-based society with liability lawyers always looking for work, there are *lots* of opportunities for litigation here... So we hide from the problem, and call it 'computer error' instead – make out that "the computer did it to us" – so somehow it's *no-one's* responsibility, because it's conveniently outside of everyone's apparent boundaries.

> This kind of 'game-play' with boundaries, incidentally, is a common 'export'-mechanism for power-under: it's also used in scapegoating, for example. The Other – here, the computer system – is first *included* within the sphere of influence, and then forcibly *excluded* by blame, to push responsibility away from Self.

Because it's shuffled onward as 'someone else's problem', nothing gets done. No-one learns. And no-one has the response-ability to deal with the issue: so it happens again, and again, and again...

Yet if we take a true system-view of the situation, the *real* system isn't just the computer, or the network, or the operators, or the training manuals, or whatever: it's *all* of it – the way everything interacts within that overall task. A 'system error' occurs when anything fails *anywhere* within that larger system.

As software designers know all too well, most system-failures occur at the edges, the boundaries between systems. To control *anything* completely, we end up needing to control *everything*. Which isn't possible. Every system is part of a larger system – all the way up to 'the everything'. For sanity's sake, we may create supposed boundaries between systems: but we must always remember that such boundaries *are* only arbitrary.

It's also essential to remember that the only real source of power – especially the response-ability to solve new problems or find new solutions to old ones – comes from people. *No matter what the problem looks like, no matter how technical, it's always a 'people-problem'.* Tracking down network glitches, or integrating software and hardware systems: technical, yes, but it's really a people-problem. Developing strategies, designing new products, making them, marketing them: they all depend on awareness, creativity, consistency, drive – finding and supporting any of those human energies is a people-problem. We can build systems within systems within systems, we can build systems-of-systems that connect and interact with other systems-of-systems, but ultimately what those systems are *really* made up of is people, and the connections between them. In many contexts, then, the human side of systems is the only one which matters.

It's here, too, that the subject-based and object-based attitudes so common in corporate systems get to be so counter-productive. It's easy to treat people as objects or subjects, by demanding in some procedure-manual that "All staff shall...". But objects don't and can't *think* – so treating people that way guarantees that problems can't be solved, that responses can only be reactive, not proactive. And because everyone's skills and experience are different, the best way to do a task will differ with each person: so a procedure-manual's subject-based assumptions about the 'right' way to carry out every activity may get in the way. Most people are capable of working out their *own* best way of working: not trusting them to do so, not *allowing* them to do so, is not only insulting, but crushes the creativity that organisations most need from 'their' people, in order to resolve the inevitable uncertainties at system-boundaries.

Most of the methods used to 'control' people, in order to control a system, actively reduce the available ability to do work. The result is systems and work-practices that are ineffective, unreliable, inelegant, inappropriate. Trying to control every detail of every item within every system is inefficient, and ineffective: reality isn't that predictable. True, those procedure manuals and the like *are* necessary – but only to describe guidelines and recommendations for routine conditions. For anything else, each system *must* provide enough flexibility to cope with inherent uncertainty – and full support for the human side of systems.

Conditions and context

If we want people to work well, we need to provide conditions in which they *can* work well. The needs to manage physical conditions are well-documented: they're usually handled under the heading of 'health and safety at work', and covered by a vast mass of legislation – though sometimes not much thought, in practice, beyond vaguely satisfying the legal requirements. By comparison, managing *non*-physical conditions rarely even makes the agenda: there's some inconsistent and erratic legislation about harassment and discrimination, which many companies perhaps try to ignore, but that's about it. Yet it's there that so many of the real productivity losses arise, because power-over and power-under can run rampant, crushing the real 'ability to do work'.

Some of the problems arise from the way people feel in different environments. To give just one example, look at the 'cube-farm' so common in large offices. In principle, the cubicles give a measure of privacy, and relative freedom from distraction, to get on with personal work. In practice, as immortalised in Scott Adams' 'Dilbert' cartoons, cube-farms are often a disaster-area: there's no easy way to communicate other than by email (phones being discouraged as too noisy and too public), so even immediate neighbours rarely speak to each other. Genuine team-work is all but impossible. Worse, many cube-farm layouts are set up so that each person is facing away from the opening, with their back to the 'door': this allows paranoid managers spy on whatever anyone is doing, but productivity drops like a brick, because so much energy is directed towards 'watching your back'.

Every incident of power-over or power-under reduces the overall 'ability to do work'. To gain maximum productivity, we need to minimise those delusions wherever possible. And there's a lot that we *can* do to reduce them within an organisation:

- look at the procedure-manuals: even something as simple as explaining *why* a procedure should be followed will reduce the usual feeling of power-over and power-under, and increase the real power to identify and resolve boundary-conditions where the usual procedure won't work well

- take a close look at the collective persona of each team, each department: rigid conformity leads to a kind of 'group-think' which can lose touch with external reality – a problem that has killed many a company in the past

- encourage the managers and team-representatives to look closely at how much they identify with that role: if they lose themselves in the role, they won't be able to *be* themselves – which means they won't be able to find from within themselves the creativity and strength that the role actually needs

- especially, memorise those definitions of power, of power-with, of power-over and power-under: create a new habit of watching for them within yourself and others, encourage others to do likewise, and take action on what you see.

34

Even meetings become productive when office-politics and the usual panderings to overblown egos are all quietly removed from the equation...

So there's a lot we can do within the enterprise. But in the wider community, power-over and power-under are closer to the rule than the exception: look at any newspaper, any TV show, at almost all advertising... We can't 'control' any of it – but it can still seriously affect our work within the company.

> For example, look at the manager of your software development team at Perfect-Place-To-Work: she's been with the company for years, one of your best senior staff, a good worker, and one who works well with everyone.
>
> But 'out there', her twins go to Hell-On-Earth Primary School; her elder daughter's just gone missing again; her teenage son's in trouble with the police; her live-in mother-in-law has Alzheimer's. She's been kept awake all night for the third time this week by next-door's drunken partying; and her husband's just been fired from his job as sales manager for Ghastly Products Inc, as the current scapegoat for their marketing mistakes, and has to go into hospital next week for another heart-operation. For her, life at home is far from easy...
>
> The issues other staff face may well be worse. That junior clerk over there, for example, has terminal cancer and knows that he only has a few months to live. But there he is, still at his desk – because his work is one of the few things that seems stable enough to hang on to as his personal world falls apart.

Everyone has life-difficulties: it should hardly be a surprise that the problems sometimes spill over into work. More to the point, given the amount of 'export' going on 'out there' as well as 'in here', it's often amazing that people do manage so well – which confirms that the real source of power lies within people, and nowhere else. And anything we can do to support that power will help: not just them as individuals, but *everyone*, including the enterprise.

This isn't about being 'nice' to people – although that attitude will certainly help, as long as it's not based on 'lose/win'. It's more that *anything* that reduces power-over and power-under will help everyone: *everyone* wins. And that includes the enterprise: the effects ripple all the way down to an improved bottom-line. Creating conditions through which this can happen doesn't even need to cost much: all it really costs is a better awareness of what's actually going on – though that awareness can sometimes be the one of hardest of skills to achieve!

Competition and cooperation

Power isn't only about our own ability to do work: it's also about how we *share* that power with others. We start off as 'I', with all the power that we have within us. But to get further than that, we meet with others – and immediately, created by us and between us, there is 'We', a compound entity with its own persona and choices. There's a wider scope of 'Us': groupings to which we belong in a less direct way – company, church, neighbourhood, or state. And finally, there are 'Them': groupings to which we believe we *don't* belong, but with which in some way we must relate.

In practice, the boundaries we perceive between 'I' and 'We' and 'Us' and 'Them' wander all the time, depending on what we're doing and feeling and the like. And *we* make connections between them: meeting the company's chief executive in person can create – or, if handled poorly, destroy – an assembly-line worker's sense of unity with the company, a sense of belonging, created between 'I' and the more distant 'Us'. As more and more connections are made, the sense of this wider 'Us' expands outward until, eventually, there's an awareness that there's no such thing as 'Them': just a more distant kind of 'Us' that is, at core, essentially the same as 'We' and 'I'. And we can work, and play, and learn, relating with 'Them' and 'Us' and 'We', through cooperation, and through competition.

Yet here, once again, there are some massive misunderstandings. Many people in business might regard all forms of cooperation with rivals as tantamount to commercial suicide; on the other extreme, some political theorists would label all competition as inherently abusive, and hence should be banned everywhere, even in business. Yet cooperation and competition are equally essential: without cooperation, nothing much can be achieved; and without competition of some kind – if only with ourselves – nothing much new can be learned. The crucial distinction is not between competition and cooperation as such, but cooperation or competition *with* others versus cooperation or competition *against* others. In our working relationships with others, we can use either to create power, or to destroy it: the choice is ours.

As usual, most of the problems arise from attempted 'export' and the zero-sum mistake. Even the basic idea that there *is* such a thing as 'Them' arises from that mistake, because in win/lose there *must* be a supposed 'Them' to take from – someone or something other than 'Us' – otherwise there couldn't be any gain for

'Us'. And in business, there's a tendency to regard only the nearby players in a given market as 'Them', '*the* competition', and ignore those further out: but infighting in a narrow market sector can have fatal or near-fatal results for all concerned if an outside player expands their own market into the sector.

A well-known example was the fragmentation of the high-end computing market in the 1980s and 1990s by competing Unix vendors. Each vendor had their own proprietary version of the Unix operating-system that, partly by intention, would not communicate – cooperate – well with those of others. But they were so busy fighting each other for 'market share' that they failed to notice that their overall market was being squeezed by Microsoft moving in from below. Many of the big-name Unix vendors – companies like Digital and Honeywell – were all but wiped out, almost without warning, in a matter of months.

The Unix market-segment seemed doomed to extinction: its rescuer, creating a whole new Internet-related market for Unix products, was Linux – a free version of Unix, developed entirely through cooperation and non-proprietary Open Source standards. At the present time, Linux has been embraced eagerly by the few remaining Unix vendors, such as IBM and Sun – though whether they've also fully grasped the lesson about the importance of cooperation remains to be seen.

The fear of loss inherent in win/lose is a key reason why there's such a fear of cooperation: yet with so many playing win/lose, there's good reason to be wary. It's also a reason why so many people shy away from a functional understanding of power. Once we recognise that the only way that works is win/win, then in negotiations we always aim to ensure that the other should also win. But if we're up against someone who's playing win/lose, *their* aim is to win not by cooperation, but by 'making' us lose. They may try this through power-over – by bullying, perhaps, or monopolistic 'unfair business practices' – or through power-under – by 'playing victim', misusing the courts to harass us with allegations about 'unfair business practices'. But whatever way it's done, we'll be in a situation where we want them to win, and they want us to lose – which is not a good position to be...

The simplest response to this kind of situation is the quote from the movie 'War Games': "the only way to win is to not play". But often this isn't possible: it shuts us out of the business, and eventually leaves it in the hands of people who really *do* 'play dirty' – which helps no-one, given that win/lose is actually an illusory form of lose/lose. The problem is well described in an academic exercise called 'Prisoners' Dilemma': and it does point to a strategy that actually works in situations like these.

The Prisoners' Dilemma scenario is simple, yet quite realistic. Imagine that both you and your partner have been arrested by the Secret Police, and you each face a two-year jail-sentence. You're each told, privately, that if you inform against your partner, your own sentence will be reduced to one year – but your partner's will go up to five years instead. And the same will happen to you if your partner informs against you: you could *both* end up with a five-year sentence. So individually, you each stand to gain by 'ratting' on your partner; but *collectively* – the sum of both sentences – you always lose by doing so; and you *both* lose if you both betray each other. Whichever way it's played, and whoever plays it, playing win/lose here always results in an overall loss – exactly as we saw with power-over and power-under.

Despite this, if it's a once-off, and it's known that it's just once-off, almost everyone goes for the win/lose option: after all, I benefit, so what if my former partner doesn't? So much for playing fair...

But what if it *isn't* just a once-off? What happens if the scenario is repeated again and again and again, with each partner alternating as to who gets to choose first? Suddenly win/lose doesn't look such a good idea: my partner wants revenge, and this time *I'm* the one who's stuck in the slammer for the next five years...

This 'iterated', or repeated, version of the dilemma has been studied intensively in academic circles, trying all manner of ingenious tricks to come off best. Yet after decades of research, there's just *one* strategy found which guarantees the shortest sentence for any individual – and it also results in the shortest overall sentence for both. It's also the simplest strategy of all: trust, then tit-for-tat. If you start first, start off with trust: that gives you both the shortest first sentence. Thereafter, repeat exactly what your partner does: if betrayed, do the exact same as your partner, exactly once, and then go back to trust. So despite the general lack of trust, and even ethics, in business and elsewhere, and despite all the omnipresent temptations to cheat, to gain some momentary 'competitive advantage', iterated Prisoner's Dilemma shows that the *only* truly successful strategy – collectively *and* individually – is never to cheat at all. Which is kind of interesting...

As usual, the same issues repeat on every scale. One of the most common business strategies is 'cooperation against': working *with* each other for the purpose of acting collectively *against* someone else. But because the strategy's overall purpose is 'against', the overall result is a larger-scale variant of win/lose – yet another illusory form of lose/lose.

The opposite is 'competition with', where we compete with each other to improve our mutual skills, or develop ideas that none of us would have found on our own. On the surface, competition-with can *look* like win/lose, but its *purpose* is power-with, so it's win/win. Most business simulations and 'practice-grounds', for example, are a form of competition-with: they work for everyone, improving everyone's business skills

> Linus Torvalds, the creator and coordinator of the Linux project, is one well-known master of 'competition with'. His dictum "may the best code win" – appropriateness of code, regardless of the nominal status of whoever submitted it – has been cited as one of the core reasons for the success of Linux.

Some resources that we deal with in business *are* zero-sum: if they are, then yes, we may well have to compete with others for our share of them. But there aren't that many of those – even budgets often aren't as fixed as they at first appear, when all the trade-offs are fully taken into account. And competing *against* others for resources that aren't fixed – such as ideas, or people, or power, or even market-share – invariably leads into a situation in which *everyone* loses.

Few things in business really do work in the simplistic way that win/lose expects. Cooperation with competitors on standards, for example, usually expands an existing market; sometimes even deliberately giving away our best ideas – as Philips did with their designs for audio- and video-cassettes – can create a new market that benefits everyone. Competition *with* others creates ideas and innovations that make the market more worthwhile; competition *against* others can destroy a market – and everyone involved.

Competition and cooperation are necessary facts of business life. Yet how we use them is our choice, our response-ability – for 'I', for 'We', for 'Us', and for 'Them' too.

BEYOND CONTROL

Control and direction

The purpose of management, we're told, is to control the operation of the respective aspect of the business. Directives, instructions, orders, procedures: these are all tools for controlling business processes. Precise control of all processes supposedly provides certainty, and freedom from surprises of any kind.

> **Control is an operational approach in which processes
> are rendered predictable through the application of
> defined rules to the relevant factors of the process.**

This all seems fairly obvious, no doubt. What's perhaps not so obvious is that none of these 'broadcast' tools ever actually succeed in controlling anything. *None* of them: not one. Control is a myth: it does not and cannot exist.

No matter how desirable control might seem to be, the reality is that there's no way that we can truly control *anything* in business.

Peter Sengé and his colleagues at MIT Sloan School of Management illustrate this with a process they call 'the Wall'.

Cover a wall with large blank sheets of paper, to draw a diagram of all the factors you need to control, in order to bring the entire of your enterprise under absolute control.

Somewhere in the middle, mark a starting-point: the name of your organisation will do for this.

Surround that starting-point with the main, obvious factors in your business: clients, employees, suppliers, financiers and the like.

To fully control your business, you need to control all of those: so you need to add in all the factors that impinge on them, too.

You also need to add in all the secondary and tertiary factors: government agencies, new legislation and regulations, general market conditions, competitors, your *suppliers'* competitors, and so on.

Now add in the uncertainties of business: bank rates, inflation rates, changes in staff or technology, a recession, epidemic, earthquake, war.

Draw lines to show all the correlations and cross-references between all of these factors.

And keep going, keep going, adding all the factors that affect all of the other factors, until you've listed everything or – far more likely, if you've really tried to list *everything* – until you run out of wall-space.

> When you get that far, stop, and step back, and look at this wall of marks and lines. Do you really think you can control all of this? Do you think that you could write a procedure-manual to cover every bit of it?
>
> The plain, simple, inescapable answer is 'No': you can't. (But don't worry about it: no-one else can, either!) It's not just complex: it's *infinitely* complex – and hence, by definition, far, far too complex for any possible means of control.

There is no such thing as control: it's a myth, a delusion. In every science, from physics to physiology and beyond, uncertainty is a proven fact. In practice, no matter how precise they may seem, all those scientific 'laws' are no more than useful guidelines. Every engineer knows this all too well, often from painful and expensive experience: nothing in the real world ever works exactly the way that we expect. The only certainty is uncertainty itself.

So why do we think it's be any different in business? Why do people think that something as complex as corporate culture can be controlled by a simplistic set of rules and regulations? Why are so many so obsessed about control, when they know control can never be achieved? Ah, now *that's* a different issue altogether...

The real issue here isn't about control: it's about fear – fear of perceived *lack* of control. "Where there's fear, there's power", says an old saying, "and where there's power, there's fear". Wherever processes are inherently unpredictable, up pops that same old tendency again: we try to retrieve a sense of power, of being 'in control', by exporting the responsibility, and the fear, to others. So it's back to delusion-time: power-over and power-under, the toddler's object-based and subject-based perspectives on life. "We *should* be the market-leaders here"; "our suppliers *should* deliver exactly on time"; "our staff *should* do what we tell them": whenever we see that word 'should', it's likely someone's lost in a subject-based attitude – treating others as a subordinate extension of self, and exporting to *Them* the responsibility to achieve the 'should'.

> There's one important exception, though: 'should' has a valid special meaning in requirements specifications, to denote a requirement that's preferred but not mandatory.

Those 'shoulds' appear as standing orders, in the procedure manual, through all the other directives for control. By their nature these can't control anything – yet present us with a perfect-seeming excuse, every time, to 'punish' those others for failing to carry out our orders. It's not exactly honest, even though it's mostly unconscious: but it's very, very common...

It's also highly addictive, because it tries to achieve something that seems so desirable – freedom from fears of uncertainty – yet can never be achieved. And because the whole approach is based on power-over and power-under, it reduces the availability of real power and response-ability – and guarantees systems and work-practices that are inefficient, unreliable, inelegant, inappropriate and the rest. And increasingly unpopular, of course.

Some procedures, standing orders and directives will always be needed: people do need to know what to do, the boundaries, risks, needs, expectations within their work. The procedure-manuals and the like aren't wrong in themselves: it's the demands for control so often implicit within them that are the problem.

The alternative to control, but which *does* support the human side of systems, is 'direction':

Direction is an operational approach in which outcomes of processes are rendered manageable through measurement of feedback within the process in relation to a defined overall aim or purpose.

On the surface, direction looks much the same as control. But the differences are fundamental: the focus is on outcomes, not processes; and it identifies success of outcomes not by conform-ance to rules, but by measuring feedback from the *overall* context.

Most so-called 'control theory' in robotics and the like is based on direction rather than control. Although the functions operate according to predefined rules, they're also designed to respond to feedback from multiple sources, including some beyond the scope of the immediate process; and they always include limit-checks to force a shutdown if the control-process itself is 'hunting' or spiralling out of manageable range – checks that are often missing from equivalent business-processes...

A defined aim or purpose is the key criterion for measuring 'success' through direction. We provide procedures for processes, but because clarity is provided by the purpose rather than the process, we often don't need to be all that concerned about precise outcomes – in fact we might abandon the original outcomes altogether if what we observe happening is more in accord with the purpose than was the nominal intent of the process.

> We'll be looking in more depth later at the whole issue of purpose. For now, just let it suffice that having a clear overall purpose for a business makes it possible to dispense with the addictive panic of 'control', and instead rely on a more relaxed yet still highly disciplined approach to the work/play/learn/relate of business.

Without a clear sense of purpose, it's likely that *nothing* in a business is really done on purpose – it's done for whatever reason happens by in the midst of the chaos of 'control'. By comparison, a clear sense of purpose provides a yardstick that enables everything in the business to be done 'on purpose' – and profitably so. That's the difference between 'control' and direction.

It doesn't take that much to change procedures and the like to highlight direction rather than control. Procedures become guidelines rather than rigid rules: most of the content remains the same – because the work needed is still the same – but the focus shifts to outcomes rather than the exact detail of work-processes.

Treating people with respect, as intelligent beings rather than mindless robots, releases more of the human power and response-ability to create the best results they can. Explaining *why* a procedure should be followed, describing its place within the overall context, allows greater flexibility to choose between following the standard procedure or adapting its principles to achieve a better outcome. And structures that support reporting of unusual feedback from the wider world – rather than punishing anyone who brings unexpected news – will create greater adaptability in the enterprise, and faster response to market opportunities.

A good label for that 'wider world' would be Reality Department: after all, it's providing feedback from the whole of reality, rather than just the small section of it that we usually choose to see. But perhaps a better name would be Chaos Department: beyond control, yet containing within itself every choice, every chance, every possibility. It's only by letting go of control, and learning to trust and work with that chaos, that we can reach the skill and creativity upon which every business ultimately depends.

Creativity and chaos

Organisations *need* ideas: organisations live or die by their ideas, and the ways in which those ideas are expressed in practice. As discussed above, organisations also tend to want control of

43

everything: but too much control kills the creativity from which the ideas arise, and can easily kill the organisation too.

So where do ideas come from? It's not from anywhere that's owned by anyone – though whether an idea can ever be possessed is an issue we'll need to return to later. They don't come from the company rule-book: as the old phrase says, "if you always do what you've always done, you'll always get what you've always got". Instead, as Nietzsche once put it, "you must have chaos within you to give birth to a dancing star": ideas arise from within us as we create connections across the chaos.

To deal with the weird world of creativity, we need more than the usual rationality. Science depends on formal reasoning to build and test any theoretical scheme, but even there, as William Beveridge noted in his classic study *The Art of Scientific Investigation*, "the origin of discoveries is beyond the reach of reason".

Beveridge's book is one of a small handful which describe techniques and examples on use of imagination, chance and intuition in scientific research. The business community is rather better served, with proven tools such as brainstorming, Buzan's mind-mapping, Michalko's 'ThinkerToys', system-thinking and mental-model techniques from Sengé and his colleagues, and the plethora of techniques churned out by de Bono and others over the past few decades. Although all have different roles within the creative process, all are similar in that they rely on the human ability to retrieve useful items of information from the midst of apparent random 'noise', and link them to the required context. Machines can retrieve information, but even the most powerful artificial-intelligence systems are of little use in this: so far, this ability to make creative connections is still a strictly human trait.

An understanding of the work/play/learn triad – that all three are aspects of the same human power and response-ability – will help in building a better understanding of the creative process. Most creativity looks like – in fact is – a disciplined form of play, concerned with learning, creating new skills and knowledge. Yet it's also work – sometimes *very* hard work. Creativity can be like driving in fog, every sense straining to pick out the smallest hints amidst a swirling nothingness. It's like trying to see a dim star at night, demanding tactics that can seem counter to all common sense. Often, the harder we try to look, the less we can see – which can be frustrating, to say the least. In many different ways, creativity can also be enormously demanding at the emotional level – an issue often missed in business, which can cause serious damage to interpersonal relations, and even to personal health, if it's not appropriately addressed.

The stresses are more severe if the emotions are not acknowledged – particularly if the emotion is generally 'forbidden' within the corporate culture or in the wider society. In business, oddly, anger is often permissible whilst fear is not, which can result in people hiding their fear – even from themselves – by inventing anger. The underlying fear is usually some variation on a theme of 'performance anxiety', a fear that we're somehow supposed to 'know all the answers', yet we don't know what's expected, or which way to turn, or where to go to find 'the answers'. This is fear is entirely normal in the early stages of a creative process, but can still be extremely uncomfortable...

With the apparent 'need' in most business environments to appear successful and all-competent – because anything less is a target for power-over and power-under – the performance-anxiety is made much worse than it need be. I've known many competent people who are terrified that they'll be 'found out', that they'll be thought of as a fraud, and so on – not realising that everyone else is undergoing the same agonies, but no-one dares admit it. An 'outsider' facilitator, though, can reduce the stress-levels – and the angry outbursts – just by explaining that this kind of uncertainty and emotional discomfort is a normal part of the process, and that the best way to handle it is by acknowledging the feelings and the fears rather than by trying to ignore them.

Understanding the concept of response-ability helps to reduce the stress, too. Our feelings are part of who we are, so we have no control over them as such – but we *do* have choice, and response-ability, as to how we respond to those feelings. By deliberately developing awareness of our feelings – rather than hiding from them, as is so often required in business – we can develop a 'gap' between the feeling and the habitual response to that feeling, and thus create space for genuine choice, a literal response-ability. "'I' is not that which changes, 'I' is that which *chooses*": developing a sense of 'I' and the response-ability of 'I' constructs an island of calm within the self, a fixed place to stand – making it easier to manage the confusion and chaos of creativity.

The other danger is that creativity can be *too* involving. It's good to see people enthusiastic about their work, yet it's worth remembering that 'enthusiasm' literally means 'filled with God' – a kind of 'divine madness', leaving little space for anything else. In the midst of the excitement of creative work, it can be easy to forget that it *is* work, and that the often enormous amounts of energy expended on that work do need to be replaced and maintained – otherwise the inevitable result is burn-out, from which in some cases there may never be a recovery.

Although it affects all industries, the software industry is particularly notorious for its poor handling of this problem, perhaps because few understand that programming is still more art than science, and makes the same creative demands as for any other art-form. A few companies do recognise this, addressing it by enforcing 'recovery-time' in the development process, by providing technical, creative and emotional support, and by involving everyone in the process as a team rather than as individuals – in other words, by paying proper attention to the human side of systems.

It's generally safest to treat the creative process within business as a discipline in its own right, with full integration of 'work', 'play', 'relate' and 'learn'. Most techniques need to be applied in a systematic way if they are to provide consistent results. There's also little point in 'play' without purpose: creativity needs a focus, such as a new skill, a new product, a new process.

Partitioning of the practical element of 'play' from normal everyday work is usually a good idea, too, as it needs a safe space in which to risk, to experiment, to let things 'go wrong' so as to see how to make them go right. But most of all it depends on the emotional discipline of learning to trust uncertainty – accepting its weirdness, its uncomfortable chaos, and its gifts of new ideas, as inseparable components of a single business package.

Accepting uncertainty

Nothing is certain in business. If we attempt to apply rigid controls to our business, what we get is chaos; but if we turn round and accept uncertainty, and learn to work *with* it, what we get is a weird kind of order. Again, this is the same as in science: as James Gleick commented, on the new mathematics of chaos, "it turns out that behind apparent order lies an eerie kind of chaos; and behind that chaos lies an even eerier kind of order".

In the business context, Dee Hock, the founder of VISA International, coined the term 'chaordic management' to describe the deliberate structuring of management around a theme of 'ordered chaos'. Part of it is a tighter focus on operational requirements rather than roles, because an increasing emphasis on multi-skilling means that skill-sets will vary widely between people assigned to those nominal roles, leading to different overlaps between roles as people change. Procedure-manuals, in turn, need to become more flexible than in a conventional role-based structure, in part to accommodate flexible roles, but also to allow more versatility and faster response to changing business conditions.

In many businesses, almost the only aspect of uncertainty which is addressed is insurance against risk. Even there, it's often tackled solely as a checklist of known risks – fire, theft, breakdown, injury and so on – which means it's treated as a kind of certainty, if only in a statistical sense. Yet it isn't: *the only certainty is uncertainty.*

Despite all the research and effort on risk-management carried out by banks and other large corporations, we can never plan for every eventuality. To give an extreme example, whilst I was I first writing this chapter, the World Trade Center in New York was destroyed by hijacked airliners – a scenario that still seems more like Hollywood fiction than horrific fact. Fortunately, most risk-issues are less lethal, but can still be costly, and sometimes bizarre – like the day a bored child in a suburban bank-branch crashed an entire nationwide banking network by flicking a terminal power-switch on and off because he liked the patterns it made on the computer display. "If something can go wrong, it probably will": Murphy's Law, the only true law we know...

The most crucial part of Murphy's Law – yet one that's most often omitted – is the word 'probably'. It's what makes it uncertain, un-predictable. Murphy is a real law – a direct corollary of the formal scientific proofs of uncertainty. It's also no joke at all, as all of us know to our cost. But although many do take it seriously, few seem to take it seriously enough to realise there's a weird twist to it which we can turn to our advantage. If Murphy's Law really *is* a law, then it has to apply to everything – *including itself.* So "if Murphy's Law can go wrong, it probably will": most of the time, Murphy's Law cancels itself out – which is why we get the illusion that things work in predictable ways.

Even when things do 'go wrong', the definition of 'wrong' can often seem a bit blurred. Sometimes it turns out to be a 'blessing in disguise', or an end to a dubious delusion of certainty. Sometimes it can be a real opportunity, *if* we allow it to be so: as Louis Pasteur put it, "in the field of observation, chance favours only the prepared mind". Yet Murphy can take us further still, because what it *really* tells us is that things *can* work, if we let them. If we only let things work in expected ways, we're limiting our chances. Breaking free of limits is what accepting uncertainty is all about.

This view of Murphy tells us that opportunity-management is just as important as risk-management. Failure to manage success has destroyed many a thriving organisation: serious preparation is needed, for example, if a company is to survive the human stresses of doubling in size, or more, each year – as happens quite often in some industries. It's fascinating to see how few businesses have any contingency-plans for extreme opportunities: yet statistically they're just as probable as the extreme 'disaster'-risks.

> Many organisations overemphasise the negative in other ways too. "We went through enormous effort trying to work out what went wrong in Argentina", a colleague told me, "But we did nothing at all to learn from what went right in Brazil – yet our unexpected gains there were far greater than our losses in Argentina. This is supposed to be about 'best practice', isn't it? If so, something doesn't add up…"

Careful research and recording of 'best-practice' can help a great deal – though for consistency it needs to explore 'worst-practice' too. And though it's hard to put figures against the costs of missed opportunities, they really do need to be there in the balance-sheet – otherwise genuine accountability is impossible. Accountability supports response-ability: without it, over time, proactive responses will slowly fade away to nothing – and if that happens, it'll be only the destructive side of uncertainty that becomes certain.

Beyond systems

For sanity's sake, we'll often partition work into systems: but it's essential to remember that every system is part of a larger system, and that boundaries between systems can always be redrawn another way. There's no absolute reason, for example, why an organisation's work should be split along function-boundaries, such as production, sales, marketing, administration and so on. It may seem to be easier to manage that way, but the result is often vertical 'empires' with poor communication between them – and low *overall* corporate effectiveness.

Being aware of the purpose of boundaries – as a convenience, not as a 'fact' – creates flexibility to respond to opportunities, in ways that cannot exist where work is partitioned into rigid systems. As we'll see later, there's a real need for a role of 'go-between' – the generalist whose job is to communicate across arbitrary internal boundaries, and help maintain focus on overall purpose.

The only real boundary is provided by corporate purpose, which defines the overall direction for work and the limits of 'Us'. If that sense of purpose is lost, the power-delusion of 'empire-building' – in which personal importance is linked to the number of people 'controlled' rather than the work actually done – will tend to take over instead. I've seen several companies destroy themselves that way. Lack of internal boundaries can lead to the same result: many years ago I watched as a large university all but imploded as a poorly-managed experiment with cross-disciplinary courses led to spiralling administration costs, more empire-building, loss of almost half the teaching and support staff – and no cross-disciplinary students anyway.

There's a crucial difference between *efficient* and *effective* – a difference which especially applies to work-systems. Systems may seem at their most efficient when they're most tightly controlled – operating exactly as expected by the system, making the *apparent* best use of resources, and so on. Yet that 'efficiency' is often only within the expectations of the system itself. All too often, the system may be internally efficient, but not effective in terms of the *overall* purpose in which the system is just one part – as in the old joke that "everything would run perfectly if it wasn't for the customers messing up our systems"...

As we saw earlier with power and motivation, people's ability to work arises from within themselves – not from the system. And the availability of that power is something that can't be controlled from 'outside': it arises only from within people themselves. What the system *can* do, all too easily, is get in the way of that power: and it happens all too often.

Many years ago, W Edwards Deming's '85/15 Rule' indicated that some 85 percent of people's effectiveness at work is determined by the work-systems, and only 15 percent by their own skill. But perhaps a better way to look at it is that at least 85 percent of people's power – their productivity at work – can be *blocked* by a poorly-designed, over-controlling system. We can't control Chaos Department, and we can't control people: what we *can* control is the design of systems through which people meet up with Chaos Department in their work. And the systems that work best are those which provide *direction*, rather control, to allow people to work *with* the chaos, finding their power to do so from within themselves, as they alone can.

To make this possible, we need to go beyond control, beyond 'the system'. Whenever we define some kind of enterprise structure, we need to be clear *why* we're using it: hierarchies are the most efficient for speed of response, but without discipline and, especially, mutual respect and awareness of interdependence, they can easily collapse into a chaos of 'command and control'. Consensus models work well only when there's time available for consensus – which often there isn't – and when everyone knows, agrees with and commits to the supposed consensus – which often they don't. Matrix models usually manage to combine the worst of both: a multi-way hierarchy where there's no real consensus and where *no-one* knows what's going on...

Ultimately, an organisation isn't defined by its systems: it's defined by its purpose, its people and its knowledge. Systems and procedures codify knowledge into forms that people can use, but it's essential that those procedures should support the real human and practical issues rather than arbitrary conveniences. So our procedures and the like need to be flexible guidelines, not rigid prescriptions: they should never attempt to control what cannot be controlled!

ECONOMIC ACTION

The meaning of economy

The business of business – of every enterprise, whether commercial or otherwise – is economic activity. The ways in which we work, interact with each other in the process of that work, and share the proceeds of the work, combine together into what is loosely called 'the economy'.

Whenever politicians and business analysts refer to the economy, they generally use the word as a synonym for 'management of finances on a national or international scale'; yet historically the word has a much broader meaning:

> **Economy is the management of the household, in a manner which is efficient, reliable, elegant and appropriate to the respective context and scale.**

In this sense, 'the household' exists on every scale: an individual, family, company, corporation, industry, nation, the world as a whole. Originally, 'the household' was literally a family household, and 'economist' was synonymous with 'housewife'. In those days, the effectiveness of household management could make the difference between life and death. Yet over the past few centuries – particularly with the move into the cities – that housewife-role became de-skilled and denigrated in a way that has become all too familiar in other industries in recent times; material resources came more from outside the household, leading to increasing reliance on the external 'breadwinner' role. So 'economy' slowly became synonymous with how the household money was spent – hence, by analogy, with how the nation's money is spent. And that's where we are today: the old meaning survives only in the archaic and somewhat tautologous term 'home economics'.

Yet it's that older meaning that we need to retrieve if we're to gain a better understanding of what's really going on in business. 'The economy' is more than just the management of money: it's the management of the *entire* household – of everything that occurs within and impinges upon the household. As before, that applies at every scale: the 'household' of an individual, a family, a company, corporation, industry, nation, the world as a whole.

Managing a household of any kind is hard. But in business especially, money gets the most attention is because it's one of the few aspects of the economy that's easy to quantify, and provides a spurious sense of control. Yet as any home-parent knows all too well, money-management may not be easy, but it's often trivial by comparison with the people problems: and whatever the issue looks like, it's always a 'people-problem' in one sense or another.

We don't solve people-problems by pretending they don't exist – even if that may be the usual and most preferred 'solution' in politics and business. There's also an old proverb that "a fool knows the price of everything and the value of nothing": yet monetarism, for example, is one well-known political philosophy based on exactly that foolishness, with disastrous results when attempts were made to apply it in the real world of business.

Some values and qualities can *sometimes* be assigned a monetary price: but what price would you put on morale, laughter, excitement, enthusiasm for work? Even if you could invent some kind of price for any of such things, from where could you buy them? In simplistic monetarist terms, downsizing and outsourcing and the like may seem to make sense: but in the real world, the *real* economy of business, they definitely didn't – as many now-struggling downsized companies are discovering to their cost.

Some things don't have a price, but they do still have value – and thinking solely in terms of price can lead us off onto a misleading and ultimately self-defeating track.

> I remember one example, in amongst those long conversations we often have with fellow air-passengers, which illustrates this mistake particularly well.
>
> He was recently retired, he said. He'd spent his entire working life 'valuing' things – by which he meant putting a price on things. He'd got so good at it that he'd retired quite a rich man.
>
> "*Everything* has its price", he said; "if you can't put a price on something, it doesn't exist. If you don't know *that*, you don't know business". Money was the sole objective basis of economics, he argued. Feelings are "just subjective", if we can't put a price on them, we can just ignore them – they can be dismissed as "irrelevant to business".
>
> He suddenly seemed uncomfortable at that point, though. He wanted to change the subject, to talk instead about his love of motorcycles. He'd recently bought a new BMW bike, he said: he loved the quality of its workmanship, and even when he couldn't ride it, he felt a sense of pride seeing it gleaming in the garage. He felt sad that his wife didn't feel safe enough to ride it with him. It obviously meant a lot to him.

Perhaps it was a little unkind of me, but I suggested that he applied his own argument to that purchase. What was the price of his enjoyment, his pride, his sadness? According to his own logic, it was 'bad economics' to ever ride the bike, as it depreciated in value as an asset every time he rode it; in fact its monetary value depreciated even when it wasn't used, so it was 'bad economics' to have bought it at all. Yet his feelings – his own *real* values – of enjoyment, satisfaction, pride were the *reasons* for buying the bike in the first place: and thinking solely in monetary terms *destroyed* them.

A lot more of that journey passed, in quite intense conversation, before the full implications of that fact finally sunk in...

Money is only one aspect of the overall economy, at any scale of economy: yet it's by no means the central one or, in many contexts, even *a* central one. For example, most people buy not on the basis of price alone, but more on a subjective, qualitative sense of *value*. That perceived value may have little direct connection with price itself – which is why branding is so important and successful as a marketing strategy. Most people in marketing – in business in general – would know about this primacy of feeling in purchase-choices; so it's somewhat of a mystery why so few seem to grasp that the same must also apply within business itself.

Feelings are at the source of all motivation and empowerment at work: money is *one* reason why people choose to work with one corporation rather than another, but it's by no means always the central one. Most people prefer to work where they feel productive and empowered; conversely, most would avoid a workplace that's unpleasantly overloaded with power-over and power-under. Even if they can't afford to leave, they won't be able to work well in that environment; and they also won't work well if they're treated as disposable objects, or as subjects for someone's experiments in monetarist economics and the like.

So multiply that effect by a few thousand or so angry, alienated, demoralised and disempowered staff: you'll soon discover that the subjective feelings that analysts would dismiss as "irrelevant to business" can have a *big* impact on the bottom-line...

One of the original proponents of downsizing admitted recently that "we didn't often achieve the savings that we'd expected, because I guess we didn't take enough account of the human factors in our calculations". That particular 'minor error' in the economic equations has cost most downsized companies very much more than they can afford: rather too late, they've discovered that trust and loyalty do indeed have a value – and that that value which was so casually ripped

> apart and thrown away in repeated 'restructuring' may well take
> decades to rebuild.

The problem here is that it *is* hard to describe qualities and values in a way that makes sense to others – especially if those others are investors whose only interest is in short-term monetary gains. So attempts are often made to assign a monetary value to some of the qualitative aspects of business, such as goodwill, and potential intellectual property. Most of these are legally dubious, because the assigned values are impossible to prove, and can rarely be realised on the break-up of a company. Even so, many companies will assign themselves paper-values far in excess of the value of their physical assets: a multiple of five or ten times is not uncommon, especially in 'information-economy' companies in which there may be almost no physical assets at all. Yet the monetary 'valuation' of qualities is misleading in any case – much like trying to describe the comfort of a car in terms of its engine capacity.

A better solution than this kind of botched-together 'valuation' is to leave the qualities as they are, and devise meaningful measures for them. These measures will necessarily vary somewhat from company to company – they'll need to be related to the corporate purpose, in fact, as we'll see later – but even if they're only in the simple form of a subjective scale from one to ten, they'll still be more accurate and more realistic than the spurious pseudo-precision of monetary valuation.

> The SEMPER diagnostic provides a direct qualitative metric of this type
> – see the book *SEMPER and SCORE: enhancing enterprise effectiveness*,
> one of the companion volumes in the Tetradian Enterprise
> Architecture series.

The real 'bottom line' isn't just that section of the company report where the finance-figures supposedly balance out, but a summary of how the *whole* of the company's economy balances out: all of our relations with *all* of our stakeholders. This isn't just a wishful fantasy: there are now an increasing number of reporting-models which do this, such as Balanced Scorecard, or Triple Bottom Line accounting, or the Social Performance Report structures pioneered by 'values-led' corporations such as Body Shop and Ben & Jerry's Ice Cream. Or leave the standard financial report as it is, but attach a separate environmental impact statement or statement of social responsibility: that's what several large multinationals such as IBM, Volvo, Shell and British Airways already do. Either way, the aim is stop misleading ourselves and others by trying to measure everything in monetary terms, and instead describe things as they really are – the *real* economy of the business.

The financial report, in practice, is relevant only to financial auditors and analysts: potential investors will need more information than that. The downsizing debacle showed that morale is as fundamental as finance when it comes to maintaining business performance beyond the current quarter. And each corporation exists within, and as part of, the economy of the wider community. Once that's understood, it becomes clear that we need a form of reporting that makes sense to that wider community: in other words, all of our stakeholders, rather than only the shareholders.

Our stakeholders are all the people who have a stake in the quality of our work: colleagues, employees, customers, suppliers, investtors, banks, unions, regulatory bodies, industry associations, government and the community in general, and future generations too. Ultimately, *everyone* is a stakeholder in our work, if only because what we do, and the ways in which we do it, may well affect everyone. For practical reasons, it may be simpler to regard as 'the stakeholders' only those people immediately associated with our work: but we need to remember that, at times, they may include everyone.

Yet here we hit a significant problem. Everyone and anyone may be a stakeholder in our business: but in most Western nations the law in effect acknowledges just one group of stakeholders – the shareholders – as the 'owners' of the company, and assigns them automatic priority over everyone else. This is the same issue about 'rights versus responsibilities' we saw earlier, and can cause the same problems – with potentially disastrous results for operation of the business, especially in the longer term. To get much further towards expanding the productive response-ability within an enterprise, we first need to take a brief detour to rethink the end, or purpose, of ownership itself.

The end of ownership

As a concept, ownership seems obvious enough: but there's a surprising range of problems concealed within the concept – mostly to do with implicit power-over and power-under, much as we saw earlier with rights and responsibilities. To tackle those problems, we need to draw a distinction between two different attitudes to ownership: 'possession', and 'stewardship'. First, though, we need to start with a generic definition of ownership:

Ownership is an assertion of right and responsibility to exploit a resource.

In this sense, a 'resource' can be anything which is to be developed or used: a thing, a project, an idea, a skill, and so on. And by 'exploit' here, I mean 'make use of' in the widest sense, rather than solely the pejorative sense of 'mistreat' or misuse'. It's this kind of ownership that's meant when we talk about 'owning' a house, a car, a pen, or almost any other tangible object.

But in Western law, property-ownership is essentially defined as an exclusive personal right of possession. Whilst that meaning just about makes sense with physical resources, it tends to fall apart when we try to apply it to intangible resources – a hope, a fear, an idea, an expectation, and so on. Or, for that matter, to relationship-resources: all manner of confusions can arise if anyone thinks that they 'possess' their partner – or even their cat!

Unlike possession, what I've called 'stewardship' does cover management of those other resources. On the surface, it looks much like possession, because of the way that rights arise implicitly from interlocking responsibilities; but it gets there by centring on the responsibilities rather than the rights:

Stewardship is an assertion of responsibility for the appropriate management of the exploitation of a resource.

It's this sense of stewardship that we mean when we talk about 'owning up': an acceptance of responsibility – response-ability – to repair the damage from some accident or mistake in which we were involved. It's also this sense that we mean when we talk about people 'taking ownership' of a project: they're expressing a commitment and responsibility for its expression, in the most appropriate way. And it's a sense which is as aware of others' needs as of one's own: some of the Plains Indian peoples, for example, asserted that any major decision they made needed to take account not only the needs of the next seven generations, but respect for the previous seven generations as well.

Stewardship is active, in that there's always a *purpose* for the stewardship of the resource. By comparison, possession is often passive, in the sense that resources are often owned solely for the sake of having the feeling of 'owning' them – or, conversely, in order to avoid the feeling, or fear, of *not* having them in the event that we want them available. Some of the resistance to innovations such as just-in-time inventory management, for example, will arise from fear-based 'needs' for possession – the 'need' for a spurious sense of control and certainty which often leads to inefficient and ineffective use of resources.

> Another classic example of this trust-issue can often be seen in busy cafés and line-service restaurants. One person in a group will find and 'hold' an empty table for the others, preventing anyone else who's just been served from using it – even though the others in the group are waiting in line, and therefore don't *need* the table until they've been served.

There are many other contexts, too, in which a much higher throughput or efficiency can be achieved if people don't try to 'possess' resources that they don't actually need.

The other crucial distinction is that rights are personal, whereas responsibilities are social. In the sense described earlier, this is actually a spiritual issue: in part, *response-ability is the expression of the power of the self in any context which is greater than the immediate self.* There's also a related and similarly crucial distinction between 'freedom for', which is usually an expression of responsibility, and 'freedom to' or 'freedom from' – in other words 'freedom to not' have to deal with something – which, when analysed in depth, usually turns out to be a self-centred assertion of 'right' to indulge in power-over or power-under.

> Freedom is important, so it's unfortunate that most assertions of 'freedom' to do or not-do something in a commercial context generally fit into the latter category, not the former. To give just one example amongst many, the only apparent purpose of Microsoft's infamous 'Freedom To Innovate' campaign was to *prevent* innovation by others – an assertion of 'freedom to' being used to override 'freedom for'.

Most rights and freedoms are defined only at the personal level, and hence tend to incite self-centredness – the classic "what's in it for me?" attitude, often combined with a lack of awareness that others have exactly the same rights and needs. When possession is asserted as a right, a 'freedom to' without explicit responsibilities – as in most property-law – the definition we actually get in practice is this:

Possession is an assertion of exclusive right to exploit a resource, without reference or responsibility to others, either in the present or elsewhen.

And that's where the real problems start...

Stewardship arises from adult purpose, whereas possession arises from an infantile self-centredness, 'to have and to hold' – with all the toddler-stage problems that that implies. We'll see possession used as power-over: for example, we may prop up our sense of superiority over others by the 'exclusive' items we choose to buy and display. We'll see children, or adults, take hold of something not because they want it themselves, but because they want to prevent someone else from having it. In business – especially where office-politics runs rampant – we'll see someone take on a role not because they want to do the work, but because they want to prevent someone else from making a success of it. We'll see possession used as power-under – most obviously so when someone misuses a piece of equipment, and then sues the manufacturer for damages. We'll see object-based attitudes to ownership – again, most obviously when someone misuses a piece of equipment. And we'll see subject-based attitudes to ownership – such as the person who makes a complete mess in the office kitchen, and leaves it for everyone else to tidy up!

Whilst stewardship accepts the need to manage the resource as a whole, possession usually attempts to split the resource into that which is desired ('property') and that which is not desired (call it 'anti-property', perhaps), and then attempts to 'export' all the anti-property – whatever it might be – to others. For example, imagine a child demanding an ice-cream: "I want, I want, I want!" We give in, and give the child the ice-cream. In the midst of the expressions of delight and satisfaction – though often only short-term! – we're likely to hear phrases like "it's *mine, you* can't have any!": attempting to export *feelings* of 'not-having' to others, propping up the sense of self in power-over form, and justifying the 'right' to have the ice-cream by making others into 'have-nots'. Yet what happens when the child's finished? The wrapper gets dumped onto mother, or onto the ground, offloading the responsibility for that anti-property onto others, in a classic form of power-under.

> There's an old joke 'proof' that beer has negative weight. People can carry a full six-pack any distance at all: out into the bush, onto the beach, up the top of a mountain, anywhere. But as soon as the can's empty, it seems to become impossibly heavy to carry, because it's dropped at once, on the spot. A full can, it seems, is much lighter than an empty one; so *obviously* the beer has negative weight...

All of this has serious implications for business. In the past, many activities were profitable only whilst the anti-property could be concealed or – to use Douglas Adams' wry metaphor – made invisible by reassigning them as Someone Else's Problem. Strip-mining and fission-based nuclear power are obvious examples: extracting a few grammes per tonne of material, or generating vast quantities of material so toxic that it has to be sealed away safely for many times longer than recorded human history, produces an awful lot of anti-property, no matter how much we may try to make it Someone Else's problem...

> Where I lived in southern Australia, the state government has had to spend a vast amount of money every year, for decade after decade, to help clean up the mess left behind by the gold-rush of the 1850s. The total of that cost to date has already been many times more than the profit from the original mining. Yet whilst the miners may have spent their earnings in as little a week, and moved on as soon as the easy pickings were gone, the damage and repair-costs, go on forever...

It still goes on, of course, if only through ignorance, but it's not sustainable as a business-model. And the opportunities to conceal large-scale anti-property become less and less each year, as NGOs and research scientists expose more and more, and counter-export it back to the companies concerned through international standards, government regulations and, ultimately, public pressure. The same applies to non-physical anti-property: harassment at work is a criminal offence in most Western societies, and unfair contracts can be dismissed as 'unconscionable' in law.

So organisations and individuals are being forced, more and more, to take responsibility for the anti-property they tend to create: in other words, to move from a possession-based model to steward-ship. Most are discovering that, far from what they'd assumed, stewardship is *more profitable* than a possession-based one – there's less waste, and less effort expended in trying to hide the waste. But possession-based attitudes to ownership are still common everywhere, in individuals and in organisations: and for organis-ations especially, we'll see the effects of the waves of attempted export and counter-export, of all kinds of anti-property, echoing all the way down to the organisation's bottom-line – where the damage may easily lead to the death of the enterprise...

Yet the real complications arise when a possession-based model of ownership is used in a context in which there are finite limits on a large shared resource. Each 'owner' has the right to use the resource; and since the emphasis is on personal rights rather than social responsibilities, it's always to their *personal* advantage to use as much of that resource as possible.

If the limits of the resource are finite and obvious, the classic zero-sum problems arise, as we saw before. But if the limits to the resource are not obvious, and no-one appears to be responsible to maintain the *overall* resource – or if someone *is* assigned that responsibility, as steward for the resource, but is generally ignored by the owners – every user tries to maximise their personal use of the resource. "Just one more won't make any difference, but it'll make a big difference for *me*".

The result is that the resource is over-used, but the over-use is concealed for a while by delays within the overall system. Availability dwindles, as the resource loses its ability, if any, to replenish itself, or else becomes harder to find. So most individual owners then attempt to *increase* their usage in order to make up for the apparent shortfall. In time – but sometimes very quickly – the resultant feedback-loop destroys the usability of the resource, not just for a few 'losers', but for *everyone*.

This type of scenario is described as a 'Tragedy of the Commons', because the classic example is common grazing-land. Fifty years ago, the Sahel in sub-Saharan Africa was rich grassland which supported a hundred thousand herdsmen and half a million head of livestock. But it's now a bare, almost lifeless desert – the direct result of un-managed overgrazing. "Forests precede civilisations, and deserts follow them" – a comment from a Roman writer more than two thousand years ago, yet still as true today.

A Tragedy of the Commons may apply to almost any shared but over-used resource. Think of a locked-up freeway at commute-time, for example; the deluge of junk-mail clogging up the Internet; the overloaded priorities of a support-unit shared between several divisions or companies. The same is true of most mining-type operations: whether we're mining for gold, drilling for oil, clearfelling rainforest, or indulging in chemical-dependent 'farming', the resource eventually runs dry – and then all that's left is the anti-property that had been ignored throughout that process. Such scenarios cause enormous amounts of damage, in business and elsewhere, for everyone involved. They can only be prevented by emphasising social stewardship – arising from personal power and personal response-ability – rather than personal 'rights'.

A Tragedy of the Commons is the almost inevitable result of any rights-based model of ownership. Which is a problem, because it's the model that's enshrined in most Western property-law... The problems are particularly severe in business because company law enforces a concept in which the shareholders and financiers are assigned exclusive 'ownership' rights over a corporation. This concept made some sense in the days when all company assets were physical, the valuation of the company was based solely on those physical assets, and most investors had a direct day-to-day involvement in the company. But in the present day, where such 'ownership' may literally last only milliseconds, and most assets are intangible anyway, it's a dangerous anachronism – as the members of any corporation that's suffered a hostile take-over or the attentions of 'asset-strippers' will know all too well. Without responsibilities as well as rights, the current corporate concept of 'ownership' may in effect be little better than theft.

> From an anarchist perspective, all forms of property are theft; from an Islamic perspective, all forms of usury are theft; and from a Marxist perspective, virtually all business activities are theft, since profits are created only by extracting 'excess value' from individual labour or individual transactions.
>
> Such perspectives are unusual in Western business, of course, but they do have some real – if uncomfortable – validity that's well worth exploring.

That's true of asset-stripping, or most 'junk-bond' leveraged buy-outs: about all that can be said for them is that they're technically legal... They're power-over, power-under, or both, as the aim is to extract a short-term profit by destroying the corporation's overall long-term 'ability to do work' – which no-one could describe as responsible behaviour! It's also self-defeating, because asset-strippers eventually run out of prey on which to make a 'killing', and over-reach themselves: Slater-Walker, the first asset-strippers, lasted just three years before they imploded into bankruptcy; Alan Bond's paper empire lasted rather longer, but collapsed like a house of cards once it became clear that it was nothing more than an interwoven web of leveraged debts. Just as in Prisoner's Dilemma, the only tactic which works in the long-term is honesty, and responsibility: in business, the only viable end of ownership – the *purpose* of ownership – is responsible stewardship.

Here again, describing shareholders as '*the* owners' cannot make sense. It's not just that because of the 'limited liability' concept, shareholders in effect have absolute rights over a corporation, but almost no responsibilities. It's not just the speed and anonymity of stock-trading, which reduces the role of most shareholders to that of a form of gambling best described as 'punters at the corporate races'. It's not just the short-termism inherent in control of corporations by people whose only interest – both metaphoric and literal – is the current quarter's dividend. It's not just that most stock-analysts still deprecate long-term rather than short-term profits, so any moves towards long-term effectiveness can lead to destruction of a company by its 'owners'. All of these are serious in themselves; but the real problem is that, given that most of the assets are intangibles, and the bulk of those intangibles reside in people, the shareholders in principle purport to 'own' the people of the company – which is not only absurd, but really *is* illegal.

Businesses now are not commodities, but *communities*. As Charles Handy, the British business commentator, put it in his essay 'A Company Possessed?', "I believe that the whole concept of owning a company is, today, misplaced. Buildings one can own, or land, or materials, but companies today are much more than these physical things – they are quintessentially collections of people adding value to material things. It is not appropriate to 'own' collections of people. Particularly it is inappropriate for anonymous outsiders to own these far from anonymous people." Possession – ownership without responsibility – is not an appropriate model for governance of a business: but stewardship is.

It's not only that 'responsibility-free' possession is wrong in a moral sense, as Handy argued. It's more that it simply doesn't work, in terms of *overall* efficiency and effectiveness in resource-use, and *overall* profitability in that wider sense of economy. Some nations – notably Germany and Japan – require corporate boards to be made up not only of major shareholders, but representatives for employees and other stakeholders. Companies there tend to be more stable, and much more profitable in the long-term, than their shareholder-'owned' counterparts in other countries. The damage caused to corporations by the present system of Western company law is so evident and so severe that Handy and other respected business writers, such as Peter Block and Stephen Covey in the US, have called for major reform, to move the legal structure to something much closer to a stewardship-model.

Those changes will happen eventually – either that, or the entire system will break down into a chaos of infighting, which no-one in business would want. Yet the law moves slowly: significant change is unlikely to happen in the near future, however urgent the need may be. In the meantime, few companies – especially publicly-quoted ones – can risk much surface change: the short-termism inherent in the current systems of the Stock Exchange will quickly penalise any who try to go it on their own.

But at the same time, no company can afford the real costs of all the power-over and power-under incited by any rights-based concept of ownership – especially within their own business. For our own profit, in both a personal and collective sense, we need to do whatever we can to reduce those human costs. We need to do whatever we can to assist ourselves and others in understanding that the end of ownership is the response-ability of stewardship – supported, in everything that we do, by a clear sense of personal and professional purpose.

Purpose, relationship, knowledge

A corporation's economic activity arises from individual, *personal* power. The only source of that power, as 'the ability to do work', is from within us as individuals. It cannot be 'taken' from others – and any attempt to do so, via power-over or power-under, reduces the availability of that power. For the reasons we've seen, the power is greatest when it can be expressed as response-ability in a purposeful way, in a context which is based on stewardship rather than possession, and one which addresses the full scope and meaning of 'economy'.

The individual motivation through which that power arises is based on feelings – particularly a spiritual need for a sense of meaning and purpose, a sense of self and of belonging to that which is greater than self, within the work as a whole. And we express that power, and response-ability, within our work, as a dynamic balance of the triad 'work/play/learn'. The simplest way to describe the power-triad graphically is as a triangular plane, with each point of the triangle representing one of the modes of power, as in Figure 1.

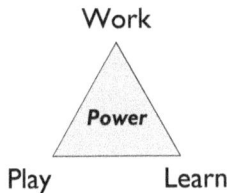

Figure 1: The work/play/learn triad

63

'Work/play/learn' is a useful shorthand term for the expression of power in general, even within in a corporate context. But it's not so descriptive about what that expression looks like in practice, in day-to-day work – and the idea that we improve productivity at work by intentionally promoting 'play' may still be a bit too hard for many managers to swallow!

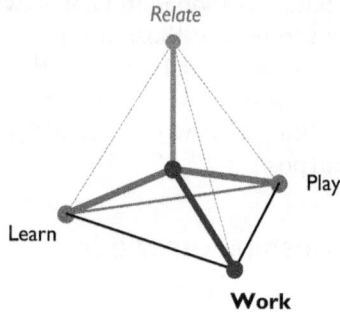

Figure 2: Work/play/learn triad expanded to tetradian

So we also need to do a brief digression into how that personal-level model of power as work/play/learn connects with that of others, as 'We' and 'Us' – and hence also as power-with. In reality, although it's how we experience power at the personal level, power is not just work/play/learn: there's another whole dimension, which we could label '*relate*' (see Figure 2). It's not that 'relate' doesn't exist at the individual level, it's more that there's no-one else – there's only 'I' – so in effect it's hidden from our awareness:

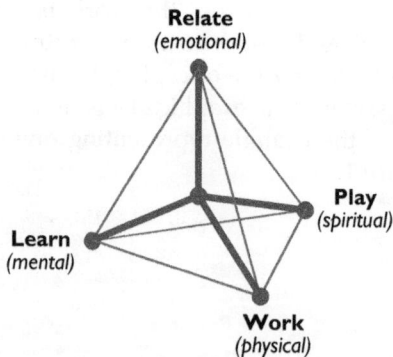

Figure 3: Tetradian linked to power-modes

In this sense, that metaphorical triangle of work/play/learn becomes a tetrahedron, a *tetradian* (see Figure 3) whose four axes map with the traditional concept of four layers of experience: physical, emotional, mental, spiritual. (As before, the term 'spiritual' here represents that 'sense of meaning and purpose, a sense of self and of that which is greater than self', in which what's loosely called 'play' itself plays a major part.)

It also maps closely with Jung's four 'functions' – Sensing, Feeling, Thinking and Intuiting – that provide the theoretical model for the MBTI, the well-known Myers-Briggs Type Indicator. But as Jung's model indicates, in each individual, and in each context, one of the four dimensions will usually be emphasised strongly, with two of the others rather less present, and one – the so-called 'inferior function' – often barely present at all.

The inferior function will often be seen as *opposed to* the primary function, with the other two functions providing some sort of balance. 'Integration' occurs, says Jung, when the inferior function is fully included in the self, and no longer experienced as opposed to the primary. By reducing those internal battles within the self, the full personal power is released, and becomes available to be shared with others, in work / play / learn / relate. So if we want maximum productivity from the people in our organisations, this is more than mere theory: this is of real, *practical* importance.

The combination of primary, secondary and tertiary functions creates a metaphorical triangle, with the inferior function 'hidden' from the self, as we saw with 'relate' in that 'self-centred' personal-level model of power. And each individual has their own primary focus, their own 'triangle of power': for some it might be learn/relate/play (academics, perhaps), or play/relate/learn (team-sports, for example), or relate/work/play (common in contexts where there's a strong social culture and strong resistance to change).

But the same is true at a collective level. Groups and organisations have their own *collective* primary, secondary, tertiary and inferior functions. And by definition, most organisations are likely to have 'work' as their collective primary function: an enterprise is *defined* by its purpose, its relationships and its knowledge. So the most common triad in organisations is work / relate / learn – which means that 'play' is most likely to be the inferior function that's regarded as the antithesis or 'enemy' of collective power (see Figure 4):

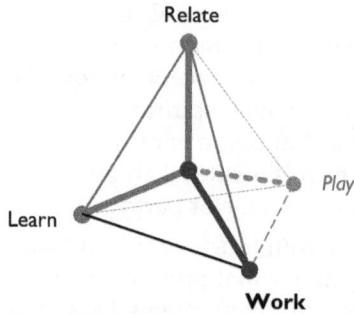

Figure 4: Tetradian and organisational triad

And that's exactly what we see in most organisations: "you come here to work, not play!" Yet unless we *do* integrate the 'play' element into the organisation in some constructive way, the available power automatically fades away: not because people are obstructive, or whatever, but simply because their full 'ability to do work' depends – in fact *arises* from – the spiritual layer of self which that 'play' element represents.

This is far from trivial: it's in no way abstract. Yet it's probably easiest to understand if we use different labels for those three other 'visible' elements of power, and describe work/relate/learn in terms that match more closely to the general business context.

So the 'work' element, or mode, or dimension, or whatever we want to call it, is represented as *purpose-fulfilment*: the various ways and means through which we fulfil our stated purpose. Most of the more-visible aspects of a corporation's economic activity – production, purchases, sales, marketing and the like – have a strong emphasis on purpose-fulfilment.

> The 'play' element comes in here as 'play-to-do' or 'play-for-a-purpose', which brings the self into the work of the organisation, usually through what's commonly described as 'work satisfaction'.

The 'relate' element corresponds to *relationship-management*: development and monitoring of how, individually and collectively, we relate with others both within and 'outside' the company.

> The 'play' element comes in here as 'play-with', which helps to build mutual relationships based on mutual respect; its absence is described by the common adage that "people join companies, and leave unpleasant colleagues"...

Externally, sales, purchasing and marketing all have a strong relationship-management component; likewise training and the inappropriately-named 'human resources', internally within the company. Skills-development – as distinct from training – also requires strong emphasis on management of relationship with *self* more than with others.

The 'learn' element is embodied as *knowledge-technology*: creation and management of knowledge – general, industry-specific and organisation-specific – and its expression through personal skill and awareness.

> The 'play' element comes in here as 'play-to-learn' or 'play-as-practice', which also brings the self into the shared-learning of the organisation.

'Technology' here is *any* system of structured techniques to develop and maintain knowledge, with equal emphasis on the human and technical aspects. In this sense, mentoring, informal education, the library, the office canteen and the water-cooler are just as important as computer networks and automated 'knowledge management' tools in the overall knowledge-technology of the enterprise. So in a business context, the work/relate/learn triad takes the form shown in Figure 5.

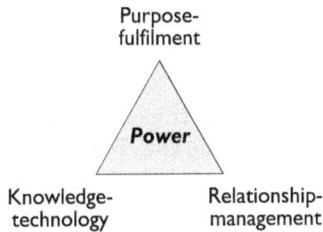

Purpose-fulfilment

Power

Knowledge-technology   Relationship-management

Figure 5: The work/relate/learn triad in the business context

This triad, with the hidden dimension of 'play' above it, forms the power-base for the entire organisation, and allows us to view its economic activity *as a whole*, rather than as an assemblage of individual, isolated compartments with loosely-coupled activities. And everything that happens within and around the organisation has its own dynamic balance of work/relate/learn, of purpose-fulfilment, relationship-management and knowledge-technology: so – as shown in the diagram below – we can map each department or work-area onto the triad in terms of the typical emphasis given to each element in the respective area (see Figure 6).

At any given time, and in any given work-area, there will be a specific emphasis for each of those three elements of power: but overall, over the entire corporation and the overall work-cycle, all three must be in balance for economic activity to take place consistently and productively – and the 'play' dimension also needs to be fully acknowledged and integrated into the other three wherever practicable.

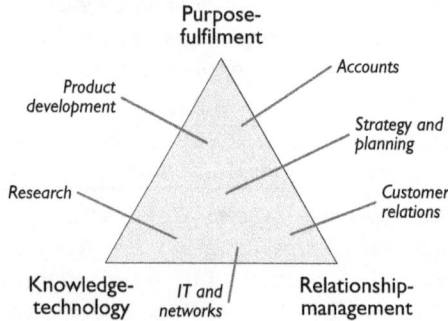

Figure 6: Business-function examples

If any department – any specific combination of work / relate / play / learn – becomes overly dominant, or weak or absent, it upsets the balance of the whole. And because the balance is dynamic, there's also a need for an explicit 'go-between' role, moving from department to department, to maintain that balance and awareness throughout the whole enterprise. Some organisations do directly support this role: in one large multinational, for example, they're referred to as the 'bag-carriers', the people who maintain organisational unity and standards. But most organisations don't – with results that can often be all too evident...

At the centre of the triad – at the exact balance-point of purpose-fulfilment, relationship-management and knowledge-technology – sits strategy, planning and review. Central to this, in turn, is the maintenance of corporate purpose, vision and values – because these set the direction for the organisation's response-ability, the expression of the organisation's collective power (Figure 7).

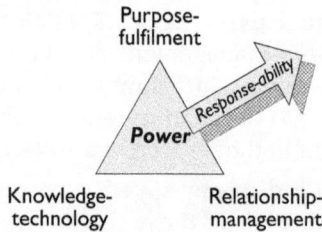

Figure 7: Response-ability provides power, purpose provides direction

The purpose of the enterprise, the context in which it fulfils that purpose, and its relationships and its knowledge, *define* that enterprise and its economic activity – far more so than any physical assets, for example, or the infamous 'org-chart'. So the remaining sections here explore in depth each of those aspects of economic activity, starting with the 'work' dimension, around purpose, and purpose-fulfilment.

FULFILLING PURPOSE

Proactive purpose

Clarity of purpose is central to success in everything that we do. In a business sense, purpose provides the basis for an organisation's existence: the motivation and meaning for 'Us', as an organised association of individuals. That'll be true regardless of whether the enterprise is commercial, political, social, non-profit, service, government or whatever. With a purpose, we can be *proactive*, watching for trends which point the way towards our purpose; but without a purpose, we can never do more than react to events. And without an explicit business-purpose, all we'll be left with is *implicit* purpose – primarily the infamous "what's in it for me?" – which is *not* a good long-term basis for business...

But what exactly *is* 'purpose', in a business context? What does purpose look like? And what's the relationship between purpose and the pointless platitudes in purpose-statements, mission-statements, vision-statements, value-statements and the like?

In practice, the *purpose* is the reason why the enterprise exists: it's as simple as that. So a *purpose-statement* is a formal statement of that purpose. It defines a direction, not a goal: something to aim for, perhaps, as an expression of collective response-ability, and something to measure against, yet not something that can be completed or 'achieved'. Then there's the *vision-statement*, which describes the organisation's vision of the wider context of the industry, the community, and society and the environment in general, within which that purpose fits – it's always something greater than the organisation itself. This is linked to, and often merged with, the *values-statement*, which identifies philosophies and social values – such as fairness, truthfulness, trust and human development – which will be upheld and promoted by the enterprise in all its operations and transactions, especially within itself.

Defining these formal statements is not something to be taken lightly, because they form the anchor around which everything that the organisation does can be assessed: as the old phrase goes, "be careful what you ask for, because that's what you'll get"!

> For more detail on the 'visioning' process, see the chapter
> 'Architecture on purpose' in *Real Enterprise Architecture: beyond IT to the*
> *whole enterprise*, another companion volume in the Tetradian
> Enterprise Architecture series.

You'll perhaps note that I haven't included *mission-statement* in the summary above. That's because, as I see it, it doesn't belong there at all – despite the fact that so many organisations proudly display them! The term 'mission' has a specific meaning in a military context, and a subtly different one in a particular group of religions, where it has a close link with 'possession' in the sense of 'being possessed by'. At a lower level, the term 'mission' does describe quite well the continuing capabilities of an enterprise, in a sense closer to 'trade-mission'. But outside of those frames, it's rarely an appropriate term to use at the core level of business, especially without vision, purpose or values to create its context.

It's not a 'mission' that we need at the organisation's core, but a clear understanding of overall purpose. In most cases, a purported 'mission-statement' is a poorly-designed substitute for a purpose-statement, rendered unusable by a subtle form of power-under embedded in its structure. At best, a mission-statement will be a purpose-statement that's been assigned a dangerously misleading label – and hence, in practice, may be more of a hindrance than a help in creating connection with purpose.

The problem is that a mission is literally a 'sending', a *single goal* – an expression of *someone else's* purpose, and for which that 'someone else' supposedly takes responsibility. In a military context, we're carrying out orders from higher up the hierarchy; in a religious context, we purport to be carrying out the orders of God. But these don't apply as such in a business context: we are – or should be – carrying out 'orders' that we *choose*, and for which we take *personal* responsibility. If a mission statement is presented as a substitute for a true purpose-statement, the effective 'purpose' is derived from an attempted export of responsibility to whoever is supposed to have defined the mission – which may be no-one...

It's true that a clear purpose has the *feeling* of a mission – the urgency, the literal 'enthusiasm' – but it's essential to understand it as a *choice*, not a 'sending'. Expressing a purpose requires personal commitment, whereas a mission is 'just following orders': so if a mission-statement is used as the core statement for an enterprise, then everyone in that enterprise is 'just following orders' for a mission for which no-one accepts ultimate responsibility – a guaranteed source of serious problems. Even worse, if and when the defined goal is achieved, the enterprise loses its stated reason for existence – which can easily destroy it.

So if all that you have for your organisation is a 'mission statement', throw it away and start again... At the least, look for the purpose *behind* the nominal 'mission', and start again from there. On the surface, it may seem small and subtle – a semantic quibble – but it's a difference that *is* surprisingly important in practice.

A purpose-statement only works if it's real, and describes a real purpose. It's said that the nominal purpose of business was "to maximise the medium-term earnings per share": but money *in itself* doesn't provide enough of a purpose to create long-term success – as even the asset-strippers found out the hard way. 'Making money' is not a purpose, but an *indicator* of successful conformance to purpose, a desirable side-effect of fulfilling the purpose – in commercial organisations, at least, since it's often a lower-priority indicator for service and non-profit organisations.

Even in commercial organisations, as we saw earlier with money-based 'valuations', focussing solely on profit rather than purpose can cause us to miss the point. As Charles Handy put it, "It is like saying that you play cricket to get a good batting average. It's the wrong way round. You need a good batting average to keep on playing in the first team." In the same way, "being the *pre-eminent* provider of 'xyz' goods and services" isn't a purpose: positioning in the marketplace is another side-effect of fulfilling the enterprise purpose, vision and values – and 'pre-eminence' is not always a desirable value, especially if caught up in the kind of 'control'-delusions we saw earlier.

A purpose-statement must be something which provides a reason and focus for work – a "reason to get out of bed on Monday morning" – and which is credible and meaningful for all stakeholders. So the overall statement needs to cover the full range of contexts of the business, from the personal to the collective, and as Stephen Covey puts it, "should deal with all four basic human needs: economic or money need; social or relationship need; psychological or growth need; and spiritual or contribution need".

As we've seen, though, the spiritual dimension is more than just Covey's 'contribution need': the connection to 'that which is greater than self' is a primary source for motivation, from which personal power – the ability to work/play/learn – and response-ability – the

72

> ability to choose and act upon appropriate responses to contexts – both ultimately arise.

Above all, what we need most in a purpose-statement is an *aim*, an overall direction of activity rather than a single predefined goal – otherwise it's a 'mission', with all the problems we've seen above. And we need it to make clear distinctions between that aim, the means and contexts through which we express that aim, and the indicators by which we identify success in that purpose.

The 'aim'-section of a purpose-statement is straightforward, and states *why* the organisation exists – the fundamental reason for the organisation's existence. In effect, it describes a vision for the *role* for the enterprise itself – whereas the vision-statement describes the organisation's vision for the wider community, which is somewhat different. Both aim and vision are addressed to *feelings*, and their function, in effect, is a wake-up call – a feeling that's strong enough to move us out of bed on a Monday morning!

The emphasis on feelings is why purpose-statements often seem like lofty platitudes. Yet that's all they *can* appear to be if all we apply is the rational mind, because it's feeling, not thought, that provides the real source for motivation – literally 'that which moves us' – and hence for personal power and response-ability. Rationality provides choice as to how to *use* that power, but not the power itself. That's also part of the reason why 'making money', on its own, doesn't work well as a purpose: to access the feelings needed for motivation, we need to connect with what we need money *for* – ultimately, feelings such as comfort, relaxation, satisfaction, and so on – rather than the money itself.

The overall aim is similar for all types of enterprise – so similar, in fact, that we could use Stephen Covey's 'universal mission statement' as a starting-point from which to explore our own aim:

The aim of all business: To improve the economic well-being and quality of life of all stakeholders.

'Economic' here means not just money – as Covey had originally argued – but that much broader sense of 'the economy' described earlier. 'Quality of life' is more difficult to define, though some aspects at least should be assessed by the measures described in the 'indicators'-section of the purpose-statement. And as before, the aim needs to describe our relationship not just with 'owners' and shareholders, but with *all* of our stakeholders – because the only way to 'win' is to ensure everyone else wins with us.

73

The 'context'-section of the purpose statement describes *how* the enterprise will work towards that aim. Unlike the aim, this will be necessarily be different for every enterprise – in fact, it's the way the enterprise distinguishes itself from others. This is where that "provider of 'xyz' goods and services" clause fits – but without any puffery about "pre-eminent provider of"... And it describes the context – usually the overall industry and specific area within that industry – in which the work of the enterprise takes place.

> For organisations in fast-changing contexts, that description needs to be generic rather than specific, and take a long-term rather than medium- or short-term view.
>
> For example, use "network interconnection facilities" – a generic market which will probably continue indefinitely – rather than "Novell / Windows-compatible hubs and routers" – a market which might well disappear after a decade or two, as names and technologies change.
>
> Involvement in industry-groups and standards-bodies – or, for that matter, community and environmental activities – might well rate a mention in this section of the purpose-statement, as they indicate the organisation's intended relations with the wider context of its stakeholders.

The 'indicators'-section of the purpose-statement describes how the enterprise will *confirm* that it's working 'on purpose'. Financial profit is one obvious indicator, a necessary one for commercial enterprises – though it may be wise to distinguish between short-term and medium-term profitability. But we also need measures for other economic qualities, such as morale, or equity, or social responsibility – particularly if we referred to those qualities explicitly in the aim- or context-sections of the purpose-statement.

Again, these measures should usually be described in generic terms: "consistent financial performance and profitability" is more appropriate than an arbitrary goal such as "a minimum 10% increase in profit each year"! The measures we specify here need to show a balance across the whole spectrum of the economic activity of the enterprise: purpose-fulfilment especially, but also knowledge-technology and relationship-management – including relationships with the wider scope of stakeholders.

That's the basic structure of the organisation's purpose-statement: aim, context and indicators. Much the same goes for the vision-statement and values-statement, though these describe more what the enterprise *is* than what it *does*. Together, they provide an iden-tifiable aim for all of the organisation's efforts: a proactive purpose for everything that the enterprise is and does.

74

Yet the organisation itself is only one side of story. The purpose-statement and the like describe the collective intent, but corporate activity arises from the personal power and response-ability of individual people – each of whom have *their* own purpose too, whether aware of it or not! That individual power becomes shared as power-with only when 'alignment' occurs between personal and collective purpose – when each person regards the collective purpose as describing a direction and focus which, at least in part, aligns with their own.

In fact, if alignment *doesn't* occur, the resultant mismatch will inevitably reduce efficiency and effectiveness within the organisation. Those inefficiencies will increase, rather than decrease, if we try to 'empower' individuals without first ensuring that alignment exists – if only in a sense of general agreement with the collective purpose. So a purpose-statement, on its own, means nothing: it's only by involving everyone in the expression of that purpose that we can access the power that it provides.

Involving everyone

Although it's short – or perhaps *because* it needs to be short – a meaningful purpose-statement can be a lot of work. It's not something that can be knocked up by corporate management over a weekend retreat, broadcast once through the organisation's intranet, and then forgotten – because that'll guarantee that it *will* be forgotten! The weekend workshop or whatever is only the start: to be of practical use, the purpose-statement needs to be discussed not just with a few key managers and shareholders, but with *every* stakeholder, to ensure that the stated purpose matches well with their own. And that really *is* a lot of work... But it's work that's well worthwhile, because a meaningful purpose is probably *the* key protection against power-over and power-under – both within the enterprise, and between it and the 'outside' world.

In terms of the classic sequence 'telling, selling, participating, delegating, co-creating', telling others about corporate purpose is only the start: it's appropriate only with stakeholders who have no direct involvement in the enterprise, or for the very first stages of potential engagement, such as in recruiting-literature. At a minimum, 'selling' the purpose to employees and other direct stakeholders is essential; but we need to make it clear, *and demonstrate*, that everyone is invited to participate in its development. It's only then that 'our people' can gain a sense of their *own* stewardship of the corporate purpose, and identify the extent of their alignment with it. Yet beyond development of an initial purpose-statement as a basis for discussion, there's not much that we can delegate to others: we can't assign the responsibility to anyone else, because the purpose identifies mutual responsibilities between the enterprise and its stakeholders – and defining those relationships is something in which every stakeholder *needs* to be involved.

In one sense, 'involving every stakeholder' is impossible, because ultimately *everyone* has some kind of stake in our business. Yet there's a lot that we can do – and need to do – with employees, shareholders, suppliers and other direct stakeholders, and with the public at large. We could use a corporate intranet or extranet to create dialogue with our direct stakeholders; to create dialogue with their indirect stakeholders, large multinationals such as Shell use mass-media advertising, public websites and 'tell-us' mail and email addresses – of which the latter at least are options that are available to even the smallest enterprise.

The main result to be aimed for is clarity on corporate purpose: 'outsiders' especially can help in this, as they're beyond the reach of internal politics. External perspectives can also help protect the purpose-development effort from the tendency toward insular, self-referential 'groupthink' within every organisation.

Although clarity on purpose is the main aim, there can be important pay-offs in other areas. For example, purpose development efforts that are open and public do help to improve relations with the general public – including those who don't choose to become directly involved. "Markets are conversations", to quote the *Cluetrain Manifesto*: creating a conversation with others about the nature of the enterprise also creates a market for its products and services. The catch is that the invitation must be real, and be seen to be real: if we invite people to a conversation, and then ignore everything they say, the only possible result is a public-relations disaster of epic proportions.

We also need to be aware that it's not just collective purpose that we work on here. Every one of our stakeholders – including ourselves as individuals – has their own purpose, each of which interacts with ours. We need to identify the extent to which we share our purpose with each of our stakeholders, to create power-with for a win/win in every interaction between us. So it's in our interest to help everyone with whom we have any kind of working relationship – especially our direct stakeholders – to identify and take stewardship of *their* purpose, to identify the respective boundaries of mutual response-ability. As James Autry put it, "the wise leader realises that the first obligation of leadership is to help people find meaning in the work, no matter what the job". This applies to our relationships with *every* stakeholder.

One result of this process is that, on occasion, we may find a serious mismatch of purpose between ourselves and some stake-holders. Sometimes the mismatch can be resolved by creative re-thinking – such as in the case of an engineer I knew, who realised that she really wanted to work with people as much as with things, and changed her involvement in the company to a part-time role. But sometimes it's time to say goodbye, no matter what the surface cost might be – as in the case of a shareholder who wouldn't accept that an enterprise could exist for any purpose other than his own personal benefit. Even so, it's still a win/win: sure, the relationship changes, but we'd no longer be carrying 'passengers' who won't accept their own response-ability in the purpose – or, worse, sabotage it through frustration, indifference or boredom!

But the people we most need to involve are ourselves. Engagement of others in the purpose occurs most through our own example: we say what we mean, and demonstrate that we mean what we say. A purpose-statement isn't just to hang on a wall, it's a description of our aim in the entire way we work. So it's not just instructions to others, as in the traditional 'top-down' style of management: it's something that we're asking *ourselves* to do – to *live* – even more than anyone else.

A purpose-statement, vision-statement, values-statement and the like is not just a commitment to a way of doing business: it's a commitment to a way of life, in everything that we do. And it's a commitment, too, to which we expect to be held accountable, by everyone – which is why we need to involve everyone in helping us to keep to that commitment.

Accounts and accountability

Identifying the vision, values, principles and purpose can be hard work. Framing them in the form of clear, concise statements is hardly simple, either. Even so, in many ways that *is* the easy part: the real work comes in translating those commitments into profitable business practice – or whatever the organisation's equivalent of profit might be. Yet despite the effort – much of it challenging, much of it embarrassingly visible to the outside world – it's still far less than the hidden costs of 'business as usual'.

Those hidden costs are not just internal, either: in the past, many an enterprise was profitable only because it could 'export' to the wider society all the 'anti-property' of the social, environmental, political and medical costs of the business. But government and the public are now more aware of those costs – and increasingly demand that businesses clean up their act, in every sense. Clarity on purpose, in all its business activities, helps the enterprise as a whole to become pro-active in addressing these issues.

Apart from anything else, choosing to be more accountable for these hidden costs is good business sense. That slogan "reduce, re-use, recycle" isn't 'tree-hugging environmentalism', as some managers and business commentators still seem to think: it's about reducing human *and financial* costs, and the real risks of a 'tragedy of the commons' scenario. Paid medical or parental leave isn't about being 'nice' to people: it's often the only way that an enterprise can protect its investment in highly-skilled staff – and *not* providing such may be the luxury that it can't afford.

Losing consumer confidence or social reputation can severely damage an enterprise, very fast indeed, as Shell discovered after two major public-relations disasters in quick succession. Hence, as one senior staffer explained, "we developed the concept of a reputation 'bank account', or reservoir – we saw we would need to make deposits there because, from time to time, there might be unavoidable withdrawals". And social activism by businesses – if it's real – can be one of the most cost-effective marketing media of all: Ben & Jerry's proved that cost-per-contact via a free festival was barely *one-thousandth* that of a single newspaper advert, let alone a whole campaign. As one of their franchisees put it, "the harder you try to blow money on seemingly unprofitable community projects, the more money you end up making".

One way to make these real is through the purpose-statement, vision-statement, values-statement or whatever – in Shell's case, their published and much-publicised General Business Principles – *and put them into practice*. Once understood and, preferably, fully committed to by all involved, these statements act as the reference point for all of the organisation's economic activity: purchases, sales, services, policies, procedures, products, production processes, choices for hiring and firing. *Everything* which purports to fulfil the organisation's purpose should be checked for alignment with the commitments made in the statements, and action taken accordingly. Sometimes it can be difficult to take that action – for example, Shell withdrew from over a hundred existing or potential business partnerships in one year alone, because of too much mismatch with their General Business Principles. But the cost of *not* doing so is even higher, especially in the longer term.

By making the statements public, we're asking others to help hold us accountable to those statements – our *choices* about the focus and direction of our business. But this kind of 'business transparency' is still rare – not least because, as most organisations with a social-responsibility focus have discovered, anyone who has the honesty to air their 'dirty washing' in public tend to get attacked, loudly, vigorously, and repeatedly.

What's actually going on in such cases is straightforward power-under – specifically, the use of scapegoating and 'other-blame' to conceal problems elsewhere, in other organisations or places. Yet it still acts as a major disincentive towards openness and accountability. The only way that this will change is if *all* organisations are measured in the same way, not just in financial terms but in social terms too. Many commentators, companies and lobbyists would resist this, of course, but the pressure is increasing inexorably: the United Nations' Global Compact and internationally-supported Global Sullivan Principles are pushing that way. New measurement models such as AA1000, Balanced Scorecard, the Global Reporting Initiative (GRI) and the Sustainability Integrated Guidelines for Management (SIGMA) also provide tools to audit economic performance in the widest sense of the word.

To audit anything, we need to be able to measure it: that's the reason for the inclusion of 'key performance indicators' in the purpose-statement. And accounting isn't a separate activity, an afterthought to tack on so as to satisfy external requirements: as Deming demonstrated many years ago, appropriate measurement, properly integrated into the respective business processes, is one of the keys to corporate quality.

Whatever we measure, it needs to be measured *in its own terms*. If our only indicator is money, we end up forcing the financial balance-sheet to carry information which isn't financial at all – leading to absurd distortions in which meaningless monetary 'valuations' for goodwill and potential intellectual property can blow out the real money-balance many times over. And although some non-monetary measures are necessarily complex, this isn't true for all: morale, for example, can be measured by something as simple as an annual staff survey.

> Other measures can be derived by analogy: in assessing return-on-investment for 'human capital', consider the 'depreciation rate' of high staff turnover, for example, or the 'downtime' of absenteeism arising from occupational injuries or low morale, or 'reinvestment' in the form of staff training and education.

From a conventional money-only model, most human issues are written down as costs. Yet ultimately, with awareness, all of them can instead be understood as potential profit-centres – and thus, for strict business reasons if nothing else, very much in the organisation's interest to help develop them, and measure them, wherever practicable.

In the real world of business, nothing is fixed, nothing is certain – and that goes for the business-purpose, too. Framing a purpose-statement is only the start of a continual process of review. All of the statements need regular reassessment, to ensure they continue to describe the real aims of the business, both from the perspective of the enterprise itself and those of its stakeholders. Accounts and accountability, in every aspect of an organisation's economic activity, are at the core of the enterprise itself: they're the means by which we ensure, continuously, that we're still on track, and fulfilling our chosen corporate purpose.

The quest for quality

In effect, the same accountability to purpose is also the core of *quality* within all of the economic activity. Quality *depends* on purpose: it's as simple as that. An explicit statement of purpose is a foundation-stone for formal quality-management processes such as TQM and ISO 9000:2000. And without a meaningful purpose-statement to anchor them, quality-initiatives will inevitably fail and fade away – regardless of the amount of effort put into them.

There's a commonly-heard comment in business that "we tried the Quality thing, and it didn't work". But the reason why it 'didn't work' is because quality isn't a 'thing': it's an attitude, or, more, a commitment to a way of life – which brings us back to purpose, and its fulfilment. As with accounting – in fact, *as* the qualitative aspect of accounting – quality can't happen if it's treated only as an afterthought to the rest of our business: *quality is the means by which we measure fulfilment of our purpose.*

And quality isn't about things, but people. No matter what the issue looks like, it's *always* a 'people problem'. Quality doesn't reside in external auditing, or in policies or procedures or the rest of the dreaded ISO 9000 paper-trail: it resides in what each person is doing, thinking, feeling, within each item of work / play / learn / relate. Numbers do matter, as a means of comparison, a measure of progress: but quality isn't about averages, percentages, mean-time-between-failure, it's about *this* item, right *here*, right *now*, in everything we say and do. Compliance to an external standard may give us a pretty logo to put on the organisation's letterhead, but it won't give us quality: we'll only get that from commitment to purpose.

Quality isn't about what to do when things are certain: it's about what to do when they *aren't* certain – as is the real case, much of the time, in real work in the real world. When we're back in Chaos Department again – when our suppliers have sent us the wrong material, perhaps, and we still have a tight deadline to meet – 'following the book' isn't likely to be much help. It's unlikely to bring us what we'd call a quality result, at any rate...

In many – most? – circumstances, what we most need is the ability to improvise appropriately. Yet there's no work-instruction for in-ventiveness or ingenuity, there's no predefined procedure which can always create creativity. But we *can* provide conditions under which they can arise. And we can also provide conditions which can prevent that creativity and inventiveness from arising – of which trying to 'keep control' by demanding that everyone follow 'the book' in all circumstances is perhaps the best (or worst) of all. It's up to us: it's *always* up to us – as individuals expressing our *own* purpose as well as the corporate one.

Attention to quality requires effort, but the result *reduces* costs. As one Toyota specialist put it, "when you orchestrate work around quality, costs take care of themselves". In their American plants, Toyota's overheads are a fraction of those in most of their US counterparts: yet the cost savings come not from lower pay or tighter inventory, but from the way that work is organised. This confirms Deming's comments, fifty years ago, that in manufact-uring, only fifteen percent of effectiveness comes from a worker's personal skill: the rest comes from the structure of the system. Toyota's work-system is structured so as to make it easy for workers to identify and correct errors as they occur: but the real focus – the *human* side of the system – is in supporting individuals to use their own power and response-ability to resolve problems and make improvements in the systems they use.

In creating conditions for quality, we do still need that paper-trail of policies, procedures, work-instructions, check-sheets and the like. But we make it work, and give it life, by giving it a purpose. Policies provide the 'why' of work; procedures identify the 'what'; work-instructions specify the 'how'; but we anchor all of them in corporate purpose, with every measurement ultimately anchored to the indicators outlined as part of the purpose-statement – and every indicator measured *somewhere* in the overall quality-system. And *everything* is anchored in personal power, personal response-ability – because individual skill and awareness is what's needed whenever anything becomes uncertain.

So successful work-instructions describe what to do when the work is routine; but they also give guidelines on when to move back to procedure, to create new – perhaps temporary – work-instructions for new circumstances. The procedures in turn provide guidelines to return to policy, to create new procedures where required; and policies provide guidelines to return to purpose – the ultimate guideline for every choice that occurs in the business. As we saw earlier, with 'right of way' in traffic law, the purpose provides the 'none of the above' clause that helps everyone retain their response-ability whenever anything becomes uncertain. Accepting uncertainty, we let go of trying to control the uncontrollable: but clarity on purpose means that we never lose our sense of direction – the focus of the organisation's business.

At the core of quality is the involvement of people in purpose. Without that involvement – or, to use Shell's term, *engagement* – we don't get quality: what we get at best is acceptable compliance to some external standard. Without the engagement of the stake-holders in the purpose, what we produce won't be perceived as quality, either: and loss of perceived quality can kill a commercial enterprise, because quality is often the only differentiator between products in the marketplace.

Markets are conversations; and as Toyota put it, quality is not a number, but a story. So our purpose provides a 'story-line' for a living story in which we, and all our stakeholders, may play their part. That's why we need to involve our stakeholders in defining purpose, because without their engagement, their commitment to that purpose, we don't have a story – or a business.

Ultimately, quality comes from people; quality *is* people. Purpose provides a focus, a story, a direction for people's individual power and response-ability. Yet ultimately we fulfil that corporate purpose not through systems, or structures, or formal statements, but by managing our relationships with all of our stakeholders – which is what we need to turn to next.

MANAGING RELATIONS

The schoolyard and the marketplace

In describing business interactions between people, the usual metaphor is a mediaeval market: bustling, busy, merchants shouting their wares, people stopping to buy – and a few dubious deals being done in the background! Few of the producers can be seen: most are hidden away out of sight, at the back of the stall, back at home, or in some foreign country. Other 'non-producers' are rather more visible: the merchants, and even their customers, at times seem to be outnumbered by the 'between-takers' – the literal translation of 'entrepreneur' – all jostling to interpose themselves in every transaction, demanding either the official excise or, more likely, their own personal cut from each deal.

We'd perhaps have to admit, too, that in that market the most common means of 'making money' – as distinct from 'making a living' – consists of misleading others about the true value of what's on offer. A cynic could easily argue that much of what goes on there is little better than 'maximising theft within the law' – with the law being fierce on small offenders, but strangely lax and lenient with regard to the richer merchants...

The metaphor still works quite well at the larger scale of the modern 'mass market'. The merchants may be multinationals, with customers perhaps viewed as mere 'consumers'. Somehow the producers remain as invisible as ever: to be seen to *do* anything, expressing personal power and response-ability in productive work, still seems to be assigned the lowest status – though no-one knows why. And there are plenty of dubious deals still going on in the background – though some of them have new names, such as 'price-fixing' and 'insider trading'. And the between-takers, the 'middle-men', are even more plentiful and persistent: and some of them have new titles, such as 'charge-card service' or 'commodity-futures broker' – or 'inspector for Inland Revenue'...

But to understand what's really going on in the marketplace and in those forgotten 'manufactories', in terms of interpersonal transactions, there's an even better metaphor: the primary-school playground – the schoolyard. After all, it's there that we each learn most of our habits for adulthood: all that's happened over the years is that those children have grown larger – and better at concealing, from others and even from themselves, those habits that are far from helpful in the real world.

So go back there to the schoolyard; take a look around in your memories. We may have thought that the marketplace was busy, but the schoolyard is even busier – so much so that even trained athletes can't keep up. Yet the hard part is that you'll see there every one of the power-problems that we looked at earlier: power-over and power-under; cooperation-against and competition-against; and object-based and subject-based attitudes to others. Much of it makes office-politics seem almost tame by comparison: "nature red in tooth and claw" indeed!

See all those metaphors for what goes wrong in everyday business, as the children teach each other their own misguided 'lessons' about power, delusion and export. Over to the right, for example, three boys are mocking the others as 'losers' – trying to hold on as long as possible to that delusory feeling of being 'the winner', even though the new game's already started. Further away, two girls aren't bothering with any of the niceties: they're in full-on screaming combat about something, feet flying, claws out, raking through each other's face and hair – surrounded by a cheering, jeering mob, each propping up their own sense of 'being powerful' by seeing others disempowered in the fight.

Closer to hand, and much more quietly, two hulking ten-year-olds are demanding a smaller child's meal-money. Over to the left, a gaggle of girls are playing the ever-popular game of 'heads I win, tails you lose' on a hapless boy, taunting him as a wimp and a coward unless he goes into the girls' toilet – and as soon as he does what they demand, they run off to the teacher to complain, demanding punishment. And off in the corner, a mixed group are plotting the downfall of a popular girl – for no reason other than that she's popular whilst they themselves are not – through that most dreaded of all forms of bullying, the carefully crafted rumour, just close enough to truth to be credible, yet also as far as possible from it, to maximise the hurt. In none of these incidents is any real power being created at all: instead, to paraphrase British humorist Terry Pratchett, it seems pleasant enough to hear and see little children at play, as long as we're careful be far enough away not to hear what they're actually saying... or see what they're actually doing to each other, and to themselves.

But of course there's also much that *does* work out well there in the schoolyard. We'll see, directly, that interweaving of work, play, relate and learn, as all manner of skills – physical, mental, verbal, emotional, social – are developed. We'll see power being created, from nowhere, as children face new challenges – many of them set by and for themselves. We'll see power-with, as children work together, play together, practice together, learn together, explore ideas together; we'll see it as an older child advises a younger one, helps another tackle a difficult obstacle, or sits with a new student to overcome shyness and awkwardness on that difficult first day at school. We'll see cooperation-with, too, as children organise themselves into teams to play a game, and use competition-with to push each other to greater skill and greater achievement.

Learning the difference between the real forms of power and the delusory forms, in relating with others, is the one lesson we most need to learn in childhood. Yet it's a lesson than many people never seem to learn – and lack of awareness of the need for that lesson, in the structure of the school and the schoolyard, tends only to make the problems worse.

That was the work/play/relate/learn of the past: yet it's still an accurate metaphor – often painfully so – for the work / play / relate / learn of the present. How to handle what happened there in the schoolyard – how to find functional power from amidst the multitude of delusions – was our challenge then: and it's still our choice now, in the muddle of the marketplace. Nothing's really changed: sure, everyone's grown up in size, but not necessarily in awareness… In any case, most of us tend to revert back towards the self-centredness of childhood when we're under stress. It's a real problem – and, as usual, it's one that we won't solve by pretending that it doesn't exist.

For most managers, managing the money-side of their part of the organisation's overall economy is easy enough: but managing people is *hard*. Yet the reason is simple: within most organisations, most of the structures for managing relations between the various stakeholders are no better than those of the schoolyard – they do little to help people find their own functional power, and often do a great deal to hinder it.

The usual attempts at 'control' – the HR 'bible', the endless edicts from upper management – lead only to a kind of chaos within which bullying, manipulation and other forms of power-over and power-under are more likely to be rewarded than reduced. All too often, it's back to the schoolyard again, with oversized egos indulging in toddler-stage tantrums, whilst everyone around them runs for cover... and anyone who's actually doing anything useful gets trampled on in the rush. The *real* 'rule-book' – the one that everyone's forced to follow, far too often – says "keep your head down; never argue with the boss; steal the credit wherever you can; trashing the competition and your colleagues is the only way to success". And productivity drops like a brick – with results that echo all the way down to a damaged bottom-line.

The chaotic confusions of corporate complexity, the muddle-headed miseries of most office-politics, the adversarial aggression of so much 'industrial relations' between management and line-employees: these things don't 'just happen' – 'business as usual' is what *creates* them. They're the direct, inevitable *results* of the usual attempts at control, and the usual failure to understand and respect the nature of power and response-ability. And it hurts: it hurts *everyone*, including the organisation, in every way. The *only* way out of this mess is to move beyond 'control', beyond 'business as usual', beyond the power-games of the playground: to re-think and rebuild entirely the structures through which we manage our business-relations – our relationships with all of our stakeholders – and reframe them around a better understanding of the *human* side of systems.

Shareholders and stakeholders

For commercial organisations, the first place where we need to do this reframing is with the shareholders, that small group of stake-holders who so often – and so mistakenly – believe that they alone are the owners of the enterprise. We've seen this issue already in a slightly different form, but we now need to make it more explicit. An enterprise consists of its purpose, its ability to fulfil that purpose, its relationships, its knowledge, and its assets. The shareholders may own – possess – the physical assets of the organisation: but *they do not own the enterprise itself*, because the physical assets are only one part – sometimes a very small part – of the overall enterprise.

Physical assets are *things*: tangible objects. Describing anything intangible as an asset can be a dangerous delusion – as millions discovered to their cost when the 'dot-com' bubble burst. A defined purpose is an aid to productivity, and may be the result of enormous investment of effort: but it's not an asset in the sense of something that can be possessed. Machines and materials to fulfil the purpose are assets: but they may not even exist, especially in an enterprise whose business-model relies on human inventiveness and ingenuity. Corporate knowledge is not an asset, a saleable commodity, unless in tangible form as 'intellectual property' – and even then its value as an asset may exist only in someone's imagination. But above all – above everything else – *people are not assets*. No matter how far we may sink into subject-based delusions – or worse, into the stupidities of slavery – people can never be assets in that crude physical sense. Their productive ability – and, especially, their creative ability – can never be possessed by anyone other than themselves.

"Our people are our greatest asset!" – how many organisations have we seen making this kind of claim? Yes, it sounds impressive, and yes, it's true that things and attributes and experiences that those people bring to the enterprise may well be its the greatest strength. Yet describing those people as assets, as 'things' that are possessed by the organisation, is a straight-out insult. Describing people as 'human resources' is an insult; placing a thin veneer of 'people-friendliness' on top of the same old HR policies and calling it something like 'People Strategies' isn't much better. And executives who expect – demand, even – that 'their' people will be highly creative and committed for the shareholders' benefit alone aren't showing much awareness of human needs – which is yet another reason why 'making money', on its own, doesn't work as a corporate purpose.

Either way, organisations and their 'owners' usually get what they ask for. Real people don't respond well to insults – and surly, disaffected, dispirited robots tend not to be very productive at all. Conversely, organisations which *do* bother to respect the human side of systems tend to be very productive indeed. But it's often depressing to see just how few 'owners' seem to understand this rather obvious point...

Regardless of what the law might say, the shareholders are not the 'owners' of the enterprise. The true owners – or stewards, as we saw earlier – are the people who make the organisation and its purpose part of their way of life.

This commitment to purpose is true of many shareholders, of course, especially in small or family companies, or those with employee stock-holding schemes: but it's less common for shareholders of large

Stewardship arises from response-ability, not 'rights'. Yet as we also saw earlier, shareholders' exclusive 'limited liability' in law means that they have almost the *least* responsibilities of any of the corporation's stakeholders – and in many cases, the least aware-ness of the effects of their actions on the enterprise as a whole. As Charles Handy and other business commentators have argued, an appropriate role for shareholders is closer to that of the banks: no more and no less than a supplier of finance – with an appropriate balance of rights and responsibilities within that role.

But because of their inappropriate 'owner' status in law, share-holders' self-centred obsession with short-term dividends is often allowed to obstruct *any* type of long-term investment – which will inevitably damage the long-term sustainability of the enterprise. Astute so-called 'investors' can safely run away at the first signs that the corporations they cripple in this way are starting to spiral into final decay, accelerating a collapse in which everyone but those shareholders will lose – as was illustrated all too well in the collapse of the giant Enron corporation.

The same inappropriate status of shareholders tends to override concerns of all other stakeholders, so much so that vast amounts of health-and safety legislation are required to enforce any respect of staff. Separate certification is often needed to ensure support for other stakeholders – for example, ISO 9000 on quality, for cus-tomers, and ISO 14000 on environmental management, for the wider community. Lack of integration between all these different systems and structures tends only to make things worse.

By any functional measure, the present system of company law can only be described as seriously insane – in every sense of the word. It all but guarantees poor productivity and poor long-term efficiency – and poor *real* returns for shareholders in general. By appearing to provide the greatest rewards to those who show the least responsibility, the present system invites and incites share-holders to act like schoolyard bullies – entrepreneurs as 'between-takers' in the worst sense of the word – and *actively* promotes power-over and power-under in the worst possible way. But it's the system that we have, which means that we have no choice but to work within its constraints, however absurd they may be.

From the enterprise perspective, in necessarily juggling the needs of *all* stakeholders, the best tool to manage the bizarre bias towards shareholders is the corporate purpose. Clarity on purpose creates a true *relationship* with shareholders – as stewards rather than 'possessors'. It assists them in understanding the long-term aims of the enterprise and the real need to create a better balance between long-term requirements and short-term returns. The continuing success of long-term-oriented ethical-investment and 'sustainable business' portfolios is at last educating the more aware investors toward a more balanced role, yet there's still a long way to go.

Most of these problems arose because of the various attempts to extend the possession-based system of property law to intellectual property (which it fits poorly), to emotional property (which it barely fits at all) and even to spiritual property (which it certainly doesn't). Intellectual property consists of *implementations* of ideas – which *can* be sold and exchanged – and their foundations *in* ideas, which *can't*, because we do not and, as yet, cannot know where they originate – identified origination and an identifiable trail of 'added value' being some of the primary keys to the concept of physical property.

Emotional property – feelings such as loyalty and respect, which move *outward* from the self – exists between people, and from a person to an organisation.

> Despite the legal fiction of 'incorporation', organisations themselves don't have feelings that can be reciprocated – though individuals *within* those organisations certainly do, and can.

It's a sense of *relationship* with another –hence is not transferable in the way the same sense as with physical property, because there's nothing to anchor it to physical reality. And spiritual property – issues such as morale, *self*-respect, a personal sense of meaning and purpose – always remains *inward* to the self. So it makes no sense at all to describe spiritual property, or emotional property, as a saleable item – even though that's exactly what's implied under the asset-heading of 'goodwill' in a financial report. Since such property may evaporate at any moment, without warning, assigning it a monetary value can only be described as financial fraud – no matter how common that kind of fraud may be.

It's essential to understand that relationships with stakeholders – many kinds of emotional and spiritual property – are at the core of every enterprise: relationships with shareholders, customers, suppliers, the general community, and within the enterprise itself. *An organisation's 'greatest asset' is not 'our people', but its relationships with those people.* A relationship is a real asset: but it's not an asset that can be 'possessed', bartered, bought and sold. And those relationships are fragile: if not treated with respect, 'our' market could vanish, 'our' reputation and goodwill could fade to nothing, or 'our' knowledge, skill, inventiveness and creativity – and relationships with others, too – will just walk out the door and go someplace else. So it's in the organisation's interest, and therefore very much the organisation's responsibility, to create and maintain those relationships.

But it's fascinating, if depressing, to see just how poorly most organisations handle their relationships. Power-under, and even power-over, are the norm rather than exception, especially in most corporate 'human resource' materials – and the organisations then wonder why they have problems with employees, customers, suppliers and other stakeholders... In the days of mass mechanisation, roles were based on single skills, so tightly defined and delineated that organisations could delude themselves into thinking that employees were interchangeable objects, that their staff were mere subjects, subordinate extensions of the corporate will; in the days of mass-markets and mass-media messages, organisations could just about get away with treating their clients and customers as 'consumer-objects'. Thankfully, those days are gone: yet many managers fail to recognise this fact – even though the organisations themselves played a major part in the change.

Customers demand customisation; and as the *Cluetrain Manifesto* indicated, they may well know more than the organisation itself does about the enterprise, and its products and services. Robot-machines have replaced most robot-work, not just on the factory floor but in the office too; so adaptability, flexibility and multi-skilling have become essential requirements, forcing roles to fit people rather moulding people into preordained 'roles-for-life'. And organisations have trimmed out the 'fat' so much – repeating the 'fewer people, better people, more work' mantra over and over again – that they may have no reserves left for the times when Chaos Department passes by. In short, people *matter* once more: they're no longer so easily interchangeable. Which means that relationship management is no longer a luxury: increasingly, it's the only means by which an enterprise can survive.

Managing relations is nothing new: for example, most large corporations use automated 'customer relationship management' tools. Yet functional relationship-management happens only

when *all* stakeholders are treated as true co-creators in the organisation's purpose, and are treated with the same respect
currently accorded only to 'high-value' customers, shareholders
and senior management. Most employee-relationship materials,
for example, need to be rewritten to emphasise mutual responsibilities – rather than the usual attempts to grasp hold of 'rights',
and foist all the responsibility, and all of the blame, onto others.

As Charles Handy put it, companies are not commodities but *communities*, and corporations are federations of such communities.
The same is true for most non-commercial organisations. So the
best way to avoid political problems in any enterprise – and
reduce the chaos created by all the covert office-politics – is to
make the politics explicit, with a formal constitution or its equivalent. And any relationship problems can be avoided by starting
from responsibilities rather than 'rights' – the traffic-law analogy
again – with the emphasis on *mutual* responsibilities.

Relationships are *human*: markets are conversations – and those
conversations can only be carried out in a human voice. Trying to
'control' each relationship – by faking a 'voice', for example, or by
limiting who is allowed to speak – leads only to trouble, and often
to the loss of the relationship. To manage the relationships in a
functional way, *everyone* needs to be able to speak in their own
voice – and may need help to *find* that voice in the first place. To
organisations that still depend on the spurious certainty of
'control', that kind of freedom can be frightening: yet it's the *only*
way that works well.

Open and closed

If markets are conversations, the best way to create a market is to
create a conversation. In business terms, that means creating open,
two-way conversations with all manner of stakeholders – clients,
customers and prospects, suppliers, shareholders, employees,
government and everyone else. Involving stakeholders *directly* in
the enterprise in this way demands a lot more openness than most
businesses are used to, yet it also creates many proven advantages
for the organisation:

- improved reputation
- improved product-development cycle
- improved time-to-market
- improved saleability of product

- improved self-marketing
- improved tolerance by clients about faults or problems
- improved service-delivery for service agencies

In most cases, all that stands in the way of those improvements is fear of uncertainty, of loss of control. Fear breeds secrecy – and secrecy is a reflex habit that applies to *everything*, as far as many organisations are concerned. Often everything in the enterprise is private, proprietary, protected, patented – yet it's rarely such a good idea as it sounds, because the secrecy can cause more problems than it solves. In any case, as *Cluetrain* demonstrates, it doesn't even work: the business *must* communicate with others – otherwise there's no business – yet there's no absolute way to control that communication. So why bother? What's the fear? It's worth exploring that question in some depth...

With the Internet, intranets, extranets, email and the Web all breaking down the old broadcast-style barriers to communication, some important information sources at last become available to the enterprise: its clients and customers, and its own employees. Historically, most organisations have shut them out, silenced them, with rules, regulations and Customer Relations departments all designed to *prevent* two-way communication – which is just plain stupid. The employees know how the products are made and services delivered, the customers know how they're are used: almost by definition, these people will know more about those products and services than do the management or marketing department – so it's wise to let them speak directly with each other, without the organisation getting in the way!

From a marketing perspective, this is far from trivial. Research-studies consistently show that customers who receive the brush-off on reporting a problem rarely come back for more, whereas customers whose concerns are addressed – *even if the problem could not be resolved* – are just likely to be repeat-customers as those who never had any problems at all. And as the Open Source movement has demonstrated, with the development of Linux and many other 'open' software projects, prospective customers who are involved in a project from its inception onwards become committed to the project's success – and are far more loyal and tolerant of problems than those whose role is that of passive 'consumers'.

Trying to keep everything closed down and controlled creates other problems too. Another word for 'proprietary' is 'possessed', with all the issues that that implies. All too often, ideas and inventions are trade-marked or patented not for the purpose of doing something useful with them – as functional power, 'the ability to do work' – but to withhold them from others, or to create a monopoly, a mandatory 'between-taker' relationship in some type of transaction.

To many people, of course, that sounds like the ideal form of business: a 'guaranteed earner' which no-one can avoid, yet costs little or nothing to maintain. But besides all the ethical and legal issues, such 'monopoly-games' don't work anyway: all they do is create a nuisance for everyone else – and a lot of ill-feeling, which is *not* a good idea in business.

> In the early days of steam, someone managed to patent the crankshaft – something *that* fundamental to almost all classes of machinery – and demanded a royalty from everyone else. Yet rather than pay up, other manufacturers made do with the cumbersome sun-and-planet gear until the crankshaft patent expired – by which time the patent-'owner' was already bankrupt.

In recent times Unisys tried this kind of game with the GIF compressed-image file format, one of the key standards for Internet graphics, and demanded a royalty from every user. Despite their undoubted possession of the patent, the resultant furore forced the company to back down, to a royalty only from producers of commercially-sold editor software – and alternative open standards were rapidly developed, in case someone else tried again to claim a cut of everyone's work on the basis of their supposedly exclusive 'entrepreneurial rights'.

> In another notorious example, the leaked 'Halloween documents' implied that Microsoft operated a deliberate policy of adding proprietary 'extensions' to existing international data-communication standards, not to add value for end-users, but solely to lock-in their users by preventing communication with open-source software built in accordance with the original standards.
>
> Microsoft then attempted to use copyright law to 'protect' its monopolistic misuse of such standards. This not only did further damage to the company's already-tarnished reputation, but led to a legal fight that put the entire international system of copyrights and patents at risk – not a wise move on the company's part...

In practice, manufactured monopolies are a variant of power-over: they invariably *reduce* the overall 'ability to do work', for *everyone*. They also reduce the overall effectiveness of creativity, because increasing amounts of effort must be expended on patent-searches and in devising work-arounds – metaphorically speaking, not just 'reinventing the wheel', but inventing yet another *alternative* to the wheel – rather than on getting the real job done.

By contrast, sharing ideas, and opening to everyone the best ideas, can be one of the best marketing strategies. Shared standards *create* markets, in which those who share the most usually gain the most of all. One famous example was Philips' publication of their design for the compact cassette, making it freely available to every maker of audio-equipment. Prior to that release, each company had its own proprietary design – a fragmentation much like that of the Unix market, as mentioned earlier – so that few potential producers had bothered to create content. Tape-machines had been used mainly for recording, and the overall market remained small. But the rapid take-up of the Philips cassette, playable on machines by many different makers, meant that it became worthwhile for producers to create content – which in turn created an entirely new market for simpler machines which could only play back prerecorded content.

The cassette design was patented – but only to prevent someone else arbitrarily declaring 'possession' rights on it, as had happened many times before. In this sense, the patent system was used as originally intended: to make the exact details of an invention 'patently obvious', for everyone's benefit. And the openness was good business in another sense, because although Philips had effectively created competition for themselves, they'd still gained several months' lead-time over everyone else – and also confirmed to their competitors, and to the general market, their reputation as one of the leading innovators in the field.

This stewardship approach to objects and ideas is sometimes described as a 'gift economy': wealth and status are indicated not by what is hoarded and withheld, but by what is given away. In a tight market, such status can be crucial in promoting relationships with customers, suppliers and other stakeholders.

The most spectacular recent success of the gift-economy concept has been the Open Source movement, in which many thousands of programmers worldwide have competed with each other – in a 'competition-with' sense – to create computer programs to be shared freely with anyone. These include the GNU/Linux operating system, the Apache web-server, the Samba file-server, the OpenOffice suite, and other lesser-known programs such as Sendmail and BIND which, together, all but run the entire Internet. At the present time, the SourceForge repository hosts almost *two hundred thousand* public software projects, which are open to everyone: a literal library of code which anyone can read, redesign and re-use for any appropriate purpose – and the exact antithesis of the 'trade secrets' so dear to so many commercial corporations.

Some of these projects – Apache being one well-known example – are directly supported by major computing corporations such as IBM and Sun, either financially or with paid staff-time, or both: yet the result is still free to everyone. It's not 'corporate altruism', or an expensive exercise in corporate public-relations: *everyone* wins. IBM, for example, gets to take part in the evolution of the world's most-used web-server software – and at a far lower cost to the company than if it tried to maintain its own competing product. True, IBM's competitors benefit too – but less so than if they were to cooperate in the project themselves, so that IBM *gains* competitive advantage in its market by apparently 'giving away' its intellectual property.

In fast-moving markets such as computer software, many companies have found that one of the best ways to create a market for their product is to give away, free and without conditions, full copies of their previous version. The same principle often applies with much more mundane products: for example, much of the early success of Ben & Jerry's was attributed to the word-of-mouth publicity arising from their free festivals and 'Free Cone Days', at which the company's founders and their colleagues hand-scooped free samples of their high-quality ice-cream.

The real assets of an organisation are not its staff, or its customers or clients, but its *relationships* with those people: and openness and inclusiveness are some of the key means by which these relationships can be created and maintained. At the same time, no organisation – especially not a commercial one – can afford to give away *everything*. Once again, a clearly-defined purpose-statement provides the best guide for this: assets which truly are central to the business purpose – such as Coca-Cola's famous formula – must remain proprietary, of course, but anything else which is peripheral to the corporate purpose is probably best shared with others. The simplest test is to assess whether 'opening up' would affect the corporate bottom-line: if doing so would improve it, or would cause no change – the most common case – then sharing with others is almost certainly the best way to go.

The value of open sharing applies particularly to generic facilities such as utility-software. Most businesses need information technology specific to their own needs: often the requirements cannot be met by off-the-shelf tools, yet the costs of developing and, especially, maintaining custom software can be prohibitive. The standard 'possession' attitude assumes that because custom software is expensive to develop, it must therefore be a saleable asset, and hence made as private and proprietary as possible. But to prospective buyers, any such software will need local adaptation to *their* needs – which is difficult, if not impossible, without access to the source-code. So as a proprietary item such software is often an 'asset' which no-one will buy – and the effort to sell it distracts effort from the organisation's primary purpose. In many cases, a better solution is to publish the software – or at least generic parts of it which are not specific to the organisation – and thus *share* the maintenance effort with others. That way everyone wins, everyone learns – whereas 'make-it-proprietary' forces everyone to develop their own tools independently of each other, wasting *everyone's* time and effort.

So here we come full-circle: the benefits of openness are evident, yet the main obstacle that stands in the way of those benefits is not technical, or financial, or legal, but a 'people-problem' – a fundamental fear about loss of control, of supposed certainty. It's a fear which is endemic in most corporate managements – mainly because of the prevalence of power-over and power-under in such organisations. To get much further, we need to address those issues, and the relationship-issues which arise from them – both in terms of individual behaviours, and organisational structures which support or suppress specific behaviours.

Personas and power-dynamics

Power-relationships are at the core of every company, every enterprise. At this stage, it's worth reiterating the definition of power we identified earlier: 'the ability to work / play / learn / relate, as an expression of personal choice, personal response-ability and personal purpose'. This may not be what people usually mean when they talk about power, in office-politics and the like: but it's the functional form of power, whereas the supposed 'power' in office-politics is often little more than a dysfunctional mess of power-over and power-under, which can only be reduced through a clear focus on power-from-within and power-with.

Much of office-politics and other intra-organisational behaviour is frighteningly childish. For example, we'll often see a nasty variant of 'musical chairs': in metaphoric terms, people running around chanting "round and round in the usual old game: I take the credit and you take the blame", until the music stops – at which point they all make a rush for cover, and scream *"it's all your fault!"* at the last person left exposed... Yet power-relationships are not so much about any individual, as the *interactions* between individuals – in other words, of the 'We' created between them.

Although we can each be directly responsible only for our own 'I', we also each contribute to the 'We' formed between ourselves and others. Yet without sufficient awareness of that mutual responsibility, 'We' tends to revert to the lowest common denominator derived from the individuals – which can be insanely self-centred and childish. Seeing each other through the filter of 'We', there tends to be an assumption that it's the other person, not 'We', that is childish: so there's a real tendency to react to that perceived behaviour in a similarly childish way – which is what leads to the chaotic mess of export and counter-export that so often takes the place of functional work-relationships.

Failure to understand the true nature of power, as individual *and shared* ability to do work, is what leads to the confusions in the first place. At the individual level, the fundamental problems are the zero-sum concept, and the common delusion that power is not so much the ability to *do* work as the ability to *avoid* it. For example, we'll often see (though more easily in others than in ourselves) a desire for 'authority without accountability', the subject-based 'right' to tell others what to do but without accepting personal responsibility for the end-results – in other words, a form of power-under. Time and time again, we'll see people playing win/lose, putting others down, on the assumption that this will automatically advance their own career – and fail to understand how much they're dependent on those others to have the power to do the work that they themselves want done.

We'll also see individual people, or entire work-cultures, lost in object-based or subject-based delusions, demanding that others should behave solely as extensions of self. For example, the so-called 'scientific management' behind the mass-production lines of the early twentieth century was based on an object-based error: it assumed that efficiency occurred only where work was rigidly partitioned into 'brain' and 'brawn' – where all thinking was done by management, assigning tasks to workers whose only role was to follow those orders without question or thought.

> "Check your brain in at the door", was how one of those 'worker-objects' described it...

In practice such mechanistic systems are startlingly *in*efficient: there are some gains from economies of scale, of course, but other than in contexts with very simple technology and a very stable market, those gains are swamped by the losses from reaction to the power-over on which the system depends, and from ignoring feedback from the factory floor. As Deming and others proved, several painful decades later, far greater efficiency and, especially, *effectiveness* can be achieved by treating a work-group not as a machine, but as a living entity. All roles within this are semi-autonomous and interdependent; a distinct 'brain' still exists, but provides overall coordination rather than step-by-step 'control'.

Another practical problem is that 'scientific management' creates a classic codependent structure. It gives managers the power-over illusion of control; it gives employees the power-under illusion of offloading responsibility to the managers; and both groups indulge in the 'right' to complain about what the others are (not) doing! Unfortunately, codependent structures provide all players with apparent payoffs whilst at the same time being highly addictive, so it can be far from easy to move toward a more stable and effective type of internal relationship. A clear demonstration of the advantages to *everyone* of relationships based on functional power and response-ability is often the only way to do so.

It's perhaps easy to label the problem as the foibles and limitations of individuals - especially others, of course - but it's usually not as simple as that. As we saw earlier with Masks, work-roles themselves acquire habits - and tend to impose those habits on whoever takes on the role.

> The Zen monk Edward Espe Brown described this process particularly well in *The Tassajara Bread Book*: "First came to Tassajara when it was still a resort. Got a job as the dishwasher, learned to make bread, soups, and scrub the floor. I could never understand the cooks. One of the cooks quit. Offered his job, I jumped in right over my head. Instantly I understood – in fact I acquired – cook's temperament. What a shock!"

Another case I remember was a colleague in a research laboratory whose role shifted from engineering-troubleshooter to manager. He failed to recognise that he was losing connection with the fine detail of each project, but still assumed that he alone had the knowledge needed to make things work, and hence delved into everything without being aware of the real consequences of doing so. In effect, he sabotaged every project he touched – but remained blissfully unaware of the fact, because his senior role meant that others were now responsible for tidying up the mess. For everyone involved, the manager was soon regarded as a danger to everyone's work: yet the real problem was not the man himself, but was, in a very literal sense, hidden behind – and within – the Mask of his new role.

Corporate culture can be a Mask in much the same way: we acquire the habits of the organisation, and think that they're our own. If those habits are based on power-over or power-under – which they often are, if only because so many organisations still base themselves on competition-against rather than competition-with – serious relationship problems become almost inevitable.

Even worse, once we put on a Mask, it can sometimes be very difficult to take it off, even when elsewhere – as the spouse of someone 'taken over' by a dominant organisational culture will often know only too well! The only practical defence against being subsumed in this way by an organisation or a role is to develop a clear sense of self – another reason why it's in the *organisation's* interest to assist its members to identify not just their relationship to the organisation's purpose, but their *own* purpose too.

The way in which work-relationships are structured also creates a kind of compound Mask. For the same 'lowest common denominator' reasons we saw earlier, these tend to default to dysfunctional forms, with one of two types being most common, dependent on whether power-over or power-under is the dominant style.

Where power-over is more common, we risk what might be stereotyped as a 'male' form, hierarchical and object-based. It's no accident that 'scientific management' was so hierarchical, given that it came out of a work-culture which was almost exclusively male. But the stereotypically 'female' form, where power-under dominates, is equally dysfunctional: it's a flat structure that purports to operate by consensus, but has no clear locus of responsibility, and is characterised by an excess of subject-based blame – "you *should have known* what I wanted you to do".

The 'male' structure is still common in large corporations: it's typified by the hierarchical org-chart, with 'power', or 'authority without accountability', defined by position in the hierarchy. By contrast, the 'female' structure is typified by a web, in which 'power' again is determined by closeness to the current centre, although – as is typical with power-under – it can be extremely difficult to tell where that centre actually *is*. This type of structure is quite common in government departments and not-for-profit organisations, though it's also the classic Mafiosi model.

By their nature – being based on power-over or power-under – *none* of these structures work well, in terms of supporting the maximum possible 'ability to do work'. In practice, the fear, backstabbing and general confusion can often reduce their overall efficiency to that of a single egotistic child – which could hardly be described as functional.

Perceptions of the enterprise can also be dangerously self-referential. If asked about the structure of their organisation, many managers would point proudly to the neat, tidy org-chart on their wall: yet that chart describes only a tiny subset of the *real* structure. Nowhere on the chart, for example, would we find the suppliers, the customers, the cleaners and contractors and other outsourced 'deployees' – all those 'outside' stakeholders on whom the company's work ultimately depends.

The organisation itself is only one system within a larger economic system – and it's at the edges of systems, the interfaces with other systems, that most of the problems occur. As multi-skilling becomes the norm, and working alliances mean that outside stake-holders become more actively involved in projects, the org-chart may cease to be an accurate guide even to the internal respon-sibilities of the organisation. Increasingly, the only approach which works well is to emphasise the enterprise as part of a greater whole, and assist staff in finding their *own* response-ability in that – with the org-chart no longer the ultimate definition of an organisation, but a guideline as to where appropriate information about aspects of the organisation's work may be exchanged.

Productive work-relationships need to be structured according to the nature of the work, in ways which provide maximum support for individual response-ability. Given those as selection-criteria, *any* structure may be appropriate. For example, despite the current fad for flat structures and matrix-management, hierarchies still remain the most effective model in high-stress contexts that depend on centralised coordination and high-speed decision-making – two key examples being electricity power-distribution, and the flight deck of an aircraft carrier.

In both those contexts, though, there is always a direct return-path available for priority feedback to the duty-manager, the admiral or whoever, from any point in the hierarchy, bypassing the normal slow upward path through the tree. The structure thus provides both the fastest means of distributing instructions, and the fastest means of collating results. There's also considerable emphasis on treating everyone as equals, regardless of roles. For example, on the aircraft-carrier, despite the rigid system of military ranks, the admiral and the cook's assistant alike may find themselves assigned to a 'foreign object detection' detail, slowly walking side by side down the length of the flight-deck in search for loose bolts and bits of wire that could puncture an aircraft tyre.

So if anyone asks whether a hierarchy, or a democracy, or a 'flat' consensus-type model, or a self-organised work-team, or whatever, is the best structure, the answer's "Yes"… It depends on the context, and may well be different in different contexts within the same enterprise. In one large research organisation I know, for example, the main structure is a hierarchy; the divisions operate by consensus; most tasks within divisions are handled by self-directed work-teams; but some support-groups with production-type roles operate locally with a hierarchy again, because it provides them with an efficient structure and a clear trail of reference and responsibility.

A key determinant around choosing an appropriate structure is whether the work is static – in other words, a continuing process where the same activities repeat, such as in bookkeeping or a production line – or dynamic – such as a project with distinct stages. Where the work is static, the best structure depends on the nature of the work, and will rarely change; but where the work is dynamic, the structure will usually need to change as the work progress – and the work-leader change with it.

One of the more interesting guidelines for identifying states within dynamic structures is the classic Chinese five-phase model. In the original model, the labels for the five successive phases in the project life-cycle are Wood, Fire, Earth, Metal and Water; in a business environment, though, it may be easier to use the equivalent labels from Group Dynamics – Forming, Storming, Norming, Performing and Adjourning or Mourning. We could also describe them as project-inception, analysis, design, production, and test and evaluation.

See the 'Five Elements' chapter in *SEMPER and SCORE* for more detail on this.

Different personalities are best suited as leaders for each different stage – which means that in many cases no one person should lead the project for the entire of its lifetime:

- In the Forming phase, the group has no real structure: it's an amorphous collection of individuals, gathered together by someone who acts as the leader.
- The Storming phase is not only where the project's work is identified, but also where the team's own interpersonal relationships are established: the natural conflicts, both of ideas and personalities, mean that this phase is often best led by a facilitator who is an 'outsider' to the group itself.
- The Norming phase is where plans and methods are defined to put the project into practice: the leadership role needed here is that of a mentor and guide.
- In the Performing phase, the project goes into production: it's here that the classic hierarchical structure is most likely to be useful.
- In the Adjourning phase, there needs to be a detailed assessment of lessons learned, of what went right as much as what went wrong: the leader here is again most likely to be an external facilitator, supporting the same team-leader as in the Norming phase.

Leadership of any kind involves additional responsibilities – especially in the difficult but necessary Storming phase. And all personal responsibilities will also involve personal challenges – which, despite the delusions of power-over and power-under, cannot be resolved by attempting to export them to others.

Responsibility is also 'response-ability'. Whether we like it or not, our own ability to choose appropriate responses – and others' ability to choose, too – will necessarily vary over time, according to the context of the work, personal response to stress at work and elsewhere, and many other factors. In designing work-structures, it's essential that we take into account the natural variations of that response-ability, in everyone.

And it's worth reiterating that power is the ability to *do* work, not to the ability to avoid it: so despite delusions of 'power', there's no point in our taking on any role unless we want to do the work – in every sense – that goes with it...

We should also reiterate that power isn't just the ability to do work: it's the ability to work, learn, relate and play, and maintain a dynamic balance between *all* of these. So despite all that so often goes so wrong, it's essential that work-relationships – the social aspect of work – are also perceived as part of play, and that play is a valid and necessary part of productive work. There's a great deal of truth in one of Ben & Jerry's early slogans, "If it's not fun, why do it?" – although, as one executive cynically commented somewhat later, the result may sometimes be little more than that "we put the 'fun' back into dysfunctional"!

Yet wherever a functional balance of work, relate, learn and play supports a sense of personal purpose in the work, it creates personal satisfaction – literally, 'enough-making' – which, in turn, results in high personal productivity, and a win/win for everyone involved. Relationships between individuals, and between those individuals and the organisation, really do matter: relationship-management is necessarily central to every enterprise.

CREATING KNOWLEDGE

The nature of knowledge

All individuals and organisations create and acquire knowledge, unique to their industry, market and purpose. For organisations, their knowledge to some extent defines what they *are*. Information is also supposed to be *the* key asset of the 'new economy' – which is why most large corporations spend a fortune on information-technology, data warehousing and knowledge-management.

Yet knowledge is more than mere information. It's built up from the content and context of information, and connections created between items of information. On its own, without context and connections to anchor it into Reality Department, information has no meaning and no use – and hence no value, either. And whilst the information-technology revolution of the past few decades has vastly increased the amount of information available to us, most is unusable – and will remain so without a systematic knowledge-technology to create meaningful connections.

Knowledge-technology isn't the same as knowledge-management – or rather, that specific area of IT that's been assigned that buzz-word. Another related term is 'experience': and as a colleague put it, "how would you store thirty years of experience in a data-base?" Most current automated 'knowledge-management' tools do little more than provide repositories for unlinked and often unlinkable information: they handle the information side of knowledge – and often do that very well – but rarely handle the connections which change that information into knowledge.

As the name suggests, databases are great for storing data, the raw *content* of information. But they struggle to handle metadata, the 'information about information' to describe its *context*; and most have no means to manage meaningful *connections* between disparate information-items – which is something at which, by contrast, people usually excel.

> For example, let's say I take a photograph of a colleague, using a digital camera.
>
> The image-file is raw data: I can store it easily in a database, or at least on some kind of file-server, and retrieve it at any time. But it's just an

image: and to anyone else – and possibly even to me, after a few months or years – it could well be meaningless.

To make sense of it, we need some additional metadata – a note describing when and where the photograph was taken, a caption that describes what it shows, and so on. This needs to be linked somehow to the original data.

On a suitable 'knowledge-management' system, I might be able to make automated connections to other image-files – for example, an extract, or a monochrome version for use in the organisation's newsletter, or to other photographs taken during the same business-trip.

Yet even the most meticulous diarist is unlikely to record in any file the kind of connections that a human could recall with relative ease: such as that a man who'd been sitting next to my colleague – who isn't even shown in the picture – had been talking about applications for the imaginary-axis in Maxwell's electromagnetic equations, which is what our organisation needs to know about right now. The image triggers a chain of associations, leading to the man's name, the unit he works for, its web-site, a phone number, and thence the contact-person we actually need.

And it's in those kinds of connections – with multiple, unpredictable steps, often linking to what *isn't* there – that the real value of information often resides.

So what I'm describing as 'knowledge-technology' is more than knowledge-management. It's as much about people as machines: storing, collating and cross-referencing data, but also encouraging and assisting people to build and maintain an intuitive grasp of information as a whole, from which those essential associative links can be created – and also to record the data, metadata and connections in the first place. It's more than just management: the techniques – and the study and development of those techniques, as a *technology* in its own right – are what really matter. At first glance, it looks like a technical issue, but ultimately, as with so much else, it's best understood as a 'people-problem'.

Yet whilst huge strides have been made with knowledge management technology, some fundamental issues often get forgotten – of which one of the most serious is knowledge lifetime. Sometimes the problem can be on the data-storage side, sometimes in the people, often in both. To give just one example, a client of mine needed to review the original data of a structural test undertaken thirty years earlier. The old research reports didn't provide much detail, so we needed to study the original data, which had been recorded on now-ancient magnetic tape. Fortunately the tapes were still readable – just – but only after baking them to get the moisture out. We then had to find a computing museum which still had equipment in working order, so that we could get the tapes transcribed. What came back was columns and columns of figures – no headings, no metadata at all – and hence no means to tell which column matched up with which sensor in the original test. The only people who might have known were either retired, or dead: it was thirty years later, and no-one had bothered to record these essential details in the meantime. It took a *lot* of work to sort out that mess... most of which could have been avoided with a proper understanding of knowledge-technology.

In some areas the rush to use the latest and greatest in information technology is actually making things worse. The Quakers – or, to give them their proper title, the Religious Society of Friends – maintain meticulous records of the Society's activities, dating all the way back to its beginnings in the middle of the seventeenth century. For the first two hundred years and more, everything was handwritten in hardbound journals – all of them as readable now as when they were first written. But with the advent of the typewriter, records were kept increasingly in loose-leaf binders, sometimes as blurry carbon-copies on poor-quality paper. With the rise of the personal computer came utter chaos: unlabelled cassette-tapes for unknown programs on obsolete computers, with printouts on thermal papers that faded and fell apart instantly on exposure to light and air. De-facto standards of the present day, such as MSWord on CD-format disks, give little long-term protection: the current programs won't read the files from the same nominal program of ten years ago, and the storage media may not remain readable even for that long.

No wonder, then, that the Australian National Library describes this period as "the forgotten generation". Paper records may be hard to catalogue and search, but the technology to read them doesn't go obsolete, and the fundamental file-format hasn't changed in a thousand years!

Another thing that hasn't changed is the human side of knowledge. The issues around creativity, communication and memory are much as they've always been, though these days some aspects are better understood than in the past, and some techniques are more developed. The crucial fact, though – and one that too many organisations forget – is that knowledge is always dependent on people. It's created by people, either directly, or indirectly with the assistance of some kind of technology. And for the most part, knowledge resides *in* people, and often *only* in people.

Which brings us back to the issues we saw in the previous section, about the organisation's relationship with 'its' people. In a fascinating inversion of Marxist theory, it's not the organisations that own 'the means of production' for knowledge: it's individual people. Hence, as we saw earlier, if 'our people' aren't treated with respect, 'our' knowledge, skill, inventiveness and creativity can just walk out of the door and go work someplace else. And there's nothing that the organisation or its lawyers can do to stop it: the most they can do is to prevent others from using some of the knowledge – in which case *everyone* loses. So it's worth taking a brief detour to have a look at those issues – and especially the much-misunderstood concept of intellectual property.

Mobile memory

Usable information is often termed 'intellectual property'. The ownership of ideas and their expression – as copyrights, patents, trademarks, brands and the like – is central to the 'new economy': ideas are often purported to be the primary assets of every enterprise. So the concept of intellectual property is supported by a huge and complex area of law: what's worrying, though, is that if we look closely, we'll find there's nothing concrete behind it. It's all imaginary: that entire system of law is 'smoke and mirrors', a series of legal fictions held together by power-over and power-under, and very little else.

That may sound like an extreme statement, but unfortunately it *is* correct – and has increasingly serious consequences for business. At a root level, even much of regular property law is suspect: in Australia, for example, the system of real-estate property-titles ultimately rests on an assertion of 'terra nullius' – that no legal system was extant before European settlement – which in international law has long been proven to be invalid.

In many other countries, the ultimate basis of the title-system is a legally dubious assertion of 'right by conquest': in England much of the system still derives from the arbitrary division of the 'spoils of war' after an invasion almost a thousand years ago. The legal basis for land-holding in most parts of the United States – for that matter, of the countries once controlled by the 'colonial powers' – is little better. Looking closely, we'll often find there's a disturbing truth in the old anarchist slogan that "all property is theft". And if such theft – however long ago, however conveniently 'forgotten' – is used as the ultimate ground for property law, there's then no defensible reason in law to prevent someone else from taking it, in whatever way they might choose.

Most of the time, this doesn't happen, because it's usually in everyone's interest to ignore the deeper problems and exchange property anyway in the usual way. But that it's more than a mere academic issue is illustrated by the legal chaos after East Germany ceased to exist as a separate state. Two equally-legal systems of title were in force, one from before 1945, one after. Thousands of Westerners rushed to claim assets they said had been theirs under the old system; yet as Charles Handy commented, in his 'Parable of a Fallen City', a quietly sad essay on Dresden, many abandoned their claims as soon as they discovered what ownership would entail, in terms of repairs and maintenance. In other words, they wanted the benefits of possession, but without any of the responsibilities of stewardship – and hence, by their *self*-focussed inaction, contributed to the continuing decay of that country. In offloading responsibility to others, possessive 'rights'-based ownership is inherently an expression of power-under – and thus, inevitably, over time, one from which *everyone* loses.

The situation for intellectual property is even worse. The three basic domains for intellectual property are copyright, patents and trade-marks – which are not only maintained independently of each other, but are different in every country, and often in every state. In all three domains, there are two fundamentally conflicting principles to determine rights of ownership: 'first in, best dressed' – priority of registration of ownership in that specific domain – and existing related use in another domain, such as in another country or another intellectual-property context.

In all cases, the intellectual-property rights are exactly as per our definition of 'possession', the dysfunctional form of ownership: an arbitrary assertion of exclusive right to exploit the resource, without reference to others in the present or elsewhen. And it's exactly as defensible as other dysfunctional forms of ownership: in other words, it's not. Enormous conflicts can arise whenever a property-holder attempts to expand their business into a different realm, or wherever a new structure is added to the system: witness the fights over 'cybersquatting' in the Internet domain-name space. In most cases, the 'winner' is the one who has the most legal clout, combining the implicit power-under of the law with the explicit power-over of coercion and threats, and in which the final assignment of 'right of ownership' arises from something dangerously close to 'right by conquest' – and ultimately indefensible in law.

It's worth remembering, as Charles Handy and others have warned, that the intellectual-property system was created to provide *individuals* with recognition and reward *in return for placing their ideas into the public domain*. Trade-marks were originally assigned more for protection of the general public – to identify counterfeit products – than for protection of 'corporate property'.

But over time, the legal fiction of ideas as property which can be bought and sold, the legal fiction of company as an individual entity which can 'own' such property, the nature of contract law which enables organisations to assert ownership of ideas created by anyone in their employ, and the notion that possessive ownership confers exclusive rights without responsibilities, have all combined to create the chaos we face today. Eben Moglen, professor of legal history at Columbia University, is one amongst many legal authorities who contend that, by comparison with other legal precedents, the current overlapping systems of patents, copyright law and trade secrets have not only become unworkable, but are close to complete collapse. In that sense, mistaken concepts of ownership now place everyone's work at risk.

Perhaps the closest legal parallel to the present situation is that of the infamous Enclosure Acts in Britain. During the mid-eighteenth century, the British government forced through legislation to ban common ownership of land – primarily to break the power of the Scottish clans. This provided a precedent for a fifty-year flurry of parliamentary activity, in which individuals paid politicians to promote private legislation – the Enclosure Acts – which allowed those individuals to 'enclose' arbitrary portions of common land, and convert it into private property.

The new ownership was literally exclusive: enclosure meant that all other owners were excluded from what had been in part their own land – and would have to pay for the new 'privilege' of being allowed to use it. So the Acts were little more than legalised theft, in that the former users received no compensation for the loss – though the new owner often had to pay a great deal in bribes to politicians and other 'between-takers' to 'legalise' the theft... As with the current domain-name system, whoever got their legislation through parliament first became the owner – regardless of anyone else's often equally valid claim. The result was, and still is, a legal mess of massive proportions.

Exclusive ownership, in this sense, is an arbitrary assertion of the 'right' to exclude others from access to some resource. Where the aim of such exclusion is to protect the resource – such as for a nature-reserve, or for sustainable agriculture or similar land-use – it's easy to defend on ethical and legal grounds. The 'ownership' is stewardship, as in the definitions earlier. But where the purpose is power-over or power-under – for destructive exploitation of a shared resource, or to enforce a 'between-taker' monopoly, as in the various attempts to assert private ownership of the human genome – it's impossible to defend on ethical grounds, and increasingly difficult to defend on legal ones.

This latter case does also apply to many trademarks. For example, Coca-Cola claims ownership of the phrase "the real thing", Ferrari claims ownership of a specific frequency of red light, Harley-Davidson claims ownership of a specific sound, a small Australian telecommunications company claims ownership of the word 'Yes' – and their lawyers will run rampant if anyone else makes use of such items. But what's the basis for such private ownership of public space? The true answer is "none": it's an arbitrary assertion of 'possession' – and in effect, a theft from the commons.

The situation is even worse with patents. The current system is so inadequate that an Australian attorney, John Keogh, was able to obtain 'Innovation Patent #2001100012' for a 'circular transport-ation facilitation device' – in other words, the wheel. He applied for the patent in order to highlight the flaws in the patent system itself: yet according to current international law, in principle he now has the right, to charge everyone in the world a fee to use of his 'innovation'. In practice, he wouldn't get far – public pressure would override the nominal rights, as was the case with Unisys and the GIF file-format. But the result is that the law itself is now clearly close to meaningless: the intellectual-property system has become so misused, and so far from its original purpose, that it's now little more than a legal fiction held together by lawyers' bluff – a fragile foundation for the so-called 'information economy'!

The other problem is the whole notion of assigning exclusive possession of ideas. For physical objects, we can establish a history of ownership, and a trail of 'added value' at each stage of its construction, all the way back to the original location of resources from which it's made. In that sense, ownership of objects is ultimately based both on ownership of land or other physical resources, and identification of *individual* ownership of resources at the time of creation – subject to additional complications, such as the concept of leasehold rather than freehold title.

But where do ideas come from? How do we establish *their* history, or the conceptual components from which each is made? How do we establish possession of the original location of each 'resource' – the content, context and connections – that underlies an idea, in order to establish possession of the ideas themselves? The short answer is that we can't – at least, not in the exclusive sense that the law needs. It doesn't take much thought to recognise that, legally speaking, we're on very shaky ground here...

Many attempts have been made to resolve this issue, such as the 'micro-payments' concept in Ted Nelson's long-running Xanadu project, or Tim Berners-Lee's 'distributed Web'. But they've all foundered on the problem of identifying the ultimate sources of any idea, and thus the list of 'owners' who would need to be paid for their part in its development and use. As Isaac Newton put it, we each stand "on the shoulders of giants": every idea depends in some way upon every other idea, through the web of connections that makes up the core of what we call knowledge. For example, Newton's 'Opticks', published in 1704, contains clear precursors to subsequent discoveries on interactions of gravity and light in Einstein's work on relativity two centuries later.

Even if we discount Jung's concept of the 'collective unconscious' – a shared pool of imagery to which everyone has unconscious access – the fact remains that parallel discoveries and inventions are common. One such example caused great upset for Newton, when he and two other contemporary mathematicians – Gottfried Leibnitz and Pierre Fermat – arrived independently at the same concept of the calculus. Behaving like a present-day intellectual-property attorney, Newton accused Liebnitz of plagiarism, and tried to manipulate the scientific societies to enforce his claim of exclusivity. In the long term, though, Newton's possessive rages proved irrelevant: he's now one of many who share credit for the discovery, and it's Liebnitz's notation for the calculus, not Newton's system of 'fluxions', that is most often used today.

So the real value of ideas arises not from who invented them, or who claims to 'possess' them, but in their *use* – and eventually anything which blocks that use is, and must be, discarded. From a business perspective, this is far from trivial. None of the attempts to extend classic physical-property models to intellectual property have really worked: they may *seem* convincing, perhaps, when a 'cease and desist' demand is framed in voluminous legalese, but none of them have any real foundation – a fact which is becoming increasingly evident to everyone involved.

And the more that organisations and their lawyers try to force the various intellectual-property kludges to work, the more risk there is that the entire edifice will come crashing down – possibly bringing the physical-property system down with it. So as with the large question-marks currently hanging over company law – particularly the anomalous rights and responsibilities of shareholders relative to other stakeholders – the best approach for business at present is a cautious 'wait and see': yet there's no doubt now that any attempt to build an entire economy on such flimsy foundations might not be a good idea...

Given the uncertainties about ownership of ideas, many organisations have tried instead to possess the 'means of production': the minds of individual employees. Many employment contracts look like a throwback to the days of slavery, claiming possession not only of every idea created in work-time, but in personal time too, and indefinitely into the future and even the past. Restrictive clauses are also common, purporting to prevent employees from ever working for the organisation's competitors, or even in the same industry. But whilst remembering is often hard, forgetting is even harder: what is remembered cannot simply be forgotten on a lawyer's demand. And once again, such contract-conditions may look impressive when couched in impenetrable legalese, but few are enforceable in practice – they're technically 'unconscionable' in most jurisdictions – although for any individual it can often be too expensive to prove that point.

> In my own case, as one of the original software developers of what's now known as desktop publishing, I broke out of a restrictive contract of this kind by writing a book on the arcane subject of water-divining – which, strangely enough, my former employers did not want to own...

The usual result is that, when subjected to that kind of contract, people simply shut down. As a colleague commented recently, after being informed that all of his doctoral research would become the exclusive property of the university, "I've stopped being able to do science any more – my heart just isn't in it". To organisations that don't understand the human side of systems, one-sided contracts look like a 'winner': but because it's a one-sided 'win', they don't actually work. In this case, by demanding exclusive possession of everything, the university gets nothing – and neither does anyone else. *The only result of power-over or power-under, in any form, is that everyone loses.*

The real intellectual property – the *use* of information – resides primarily in people's memory. In relation to that fact, organisations have only two choices: create a lose/lose by 'controlling', or create a win/win by sharing. What *does* work for intellectual property is to create and maintain stewardship, not possession: in other words, responsibilities shared with everyone, rather than 'rights' for a self-selected few. We've already seen one form of this, in the commercial advantages of sharing information with stakeholders and with competitors. By emphasising stewardship, we're also going back to the original intention of the intellectual-property system, which was to provide a fair means to encourage the exchange of information and ideas.

So where do ideas *really* come from? We have no way to tell: all that we do know is that it's not from anywhere that can be possessed – and that any attempt to possess that place costs us our access to it. Ultimately, intellectual property belongs to everyone – or else it ceases to exist. Those are some of the fundamental facts of knowledge technology: organisations and their lawyers might well prefer them to be otherwise, but that's the way it is, and it's best to learn to work *with* it!

Analysis and intuition

Knowledge is built up from content, context and connections. Content may be any kind of data: facts, figures, names, numbers, dates, places, images, all manner of other kinds of data-structures. A predefined set of connections provides metadata for some basic context: for example, a figure may be linked to its source and a date. But the use of that information is more often derived from wider connections that are *not* predefined: as part of an aggregate figure for the year, perhaps, or for the town or industry, or as a link to a newspaper article on a person's life. Knowledge and experience are more than mere information: and for real knowledge, *anything goes* as far as connections are concerned. But that's also what makes it so hard to separate out meaningful knowledge from amidst the morass of everyday information.

The standard solution is analysis: look for proof, make it all certain. But it doesn't actually work – or work well, at any rate. Murphy's Law shows we can never have enough data when we try to analyse everything: and every comparison takes time. The result is 'analysis paralysis' – and many missed opportunities. Whilst the uncertainty – the lack of clear control over knowledge – can cause a cause a great deal of angst, it's often the *un*predictable associations which provide the most value: think of all those business relationships that arise from casual conversations on flights and at conferences and those long lonely evenings in hotels a long way from home. Unlike machines, which for the most part can only follow predefined rules, we learn, through experience, to just *know* when something may be relevant.

One of the reasons why analysis doesn't work as well as might be expected is that it depends on repeatability: but in practice – in business as much as in the sciences – important connections may be made via the accumulation of small items of information, often unidentifiable, often unrepeatable. In this way, over time, we each build up a kind of *hologram* of our world, always sketchy, always incomplete. We constantly refine that hologram, through observation and experience. But the key point is that it's *never* complete, it's never entirely static – which is why we can't rely absolutely on analysis.

If we try to analyse a hologram, we'll discover it's a meaningless mess of lines: there's no apparent structure on which we can build the analysis. What works instead is to view the hologram *as a whole* - not divided up into arbitrary parts – and then provide conditions under which we can take a kind of 'snapshot' of that whole from various perspectives. Unlike analysis, the snapshot is instantaneous, so we *can* use it at the speed of business. The catch is that it depends greatly on the quality of the hologram – and on the metaphoric 'lighting conditions' that we use.

This snapshot-process has many different names: intuition, gut-feeling, heart-response and so on. It's still almost entirely a human characteristic, because – unlike analysis – there are no clear rules which a machine could use to do the same: I've only seen one artificial-intelligence knowledge-system which could use genuine intuitive-type rules, and even then it was very rudimentary in what it could do. So we're back to Beveridge's comment that "the origin of discoveries is beyond the reach of reason": the organisation's knowledge-technology needs to include full support for the *human* process of discovery. It needs to emphasise the complementary roles of analysis and intuition, with each supporting the other. And it needs to emphasise the *discipline* of intuition, observation, analogy and the like – which is where those many tools and techniques on creativity, brainstorming, mental-models and so on come into play.

There's a need for discipline here, because without it, the 'snapshot' is usually not taken from the hologram as such, but from our own assumptions and prejudices. There's a fundamental paradox of perception – Gooch's Paradox – which warns that "things have not only to be seen to be believed, but also have to be believed to be seen". So without discipline, and without awareness of the dangers of that paradox, it's easy to get caught up in circular reasoning, in which we see only what we expect to see, and ignore everything else –leading to 'groupthink', and the all-too-common error of "ready? fire! aim...". Organisations are understandably cautious about intuition, because a single undisciplined assumption could destroy an entire enterprise: as the old joke goes, "be careful about jumping to conclusions, because the conclusion you jump to may be your own!" Yet with discipline and practice, intuition is a skill that can be learnt – and, as many examples show, is the most valuable business skill of all.

The real problem is that so few organisations are willing to take the risk – and the excess of caution is what cripples the enterprise, in many different ways. The risk is not as high as it may seem, because analysis is always available as a backup, providing default recommendations in case of serious doubt. It's essential to understand, though, that analysis only works backwards, working from the known-in-general to the known-in-particular: that's why, if we rely too much on analysis alone, we get stuck on that old trap of "if you always do what you've always done, you'll always get what you've always got".

Instead, we need to remember that "the origin of discoveries is beyond the reach of reason". What happens in practice is that there's an intuitive jump from the 'here and now' to some trend pointed out by the hologram, and *then* reason comes into play, to link intuition to the rest of our experience – as Beveridge put it, "verifying, interpreting and developing [information] and building a general theoretical scheme". In practice, the main purpose of analysis is to provide us with a means to explain our intuitions to others: intuitions and the like are our *own* perspectives on the hologram, which are not necessarily obvious to anyone else!

Intuition is literally 'teaching from within': as such, it's the basis of all skill and creativity, because whilst others can help us to learn, the only people who can truly teach us anything are ourselves. Knowledge ultimately arises from the ways we combine our own experience with a sense of 'connectedness with everything' – another reason why a win/win attitude is so important, because the barriers built up through win/lose slowly close off access to parts of the hologram. Sharing ideas with others, as power-with, constantly creates new connections – and hence new knowledge.

Play is an important part of this – not only that a safe space to practice is needed for the development of skill, but that creativity flows more freely when people are having fun. Yet paradoxically, the most satisfaction arises when that enjoyment occurs within a framework of self-discipline – literally, of *self*-leadership. A discipline imposed from outside rarely works, because the purported 'discipline' is often a muddled morass of power-over and power-under; but a discipline accepted *as a personal choice* provides a means to express personal power, and share power with others.

Productive organisations focus on more than just the obvious layers of work: they invariably interweave work, play, relate and learn as part of every activity, though not always in a conscious way. The most productive organisations do so intentionally, as part of their purpose, and provide systematic support for the development of each individual to find increasing response-ability as a result. And as each person grows – learning more *in practice* about the nature of connections, the nature of knowledge, the balance of analysis and intuition, and the balance of personal power and shared power – the 'learning organisation' as a whole grows with them: and *everyone* wins.

The learning organisation

The term 'learning organisation' was coined by Peter Sengé to describe a constant process of self-education and self-development, as the foundation for an entire enterprise. It goes far deeper than the usual 'fast-fix' fads, or the shortlived 'human resource' training courses. Instead, it promotes a quiet, careful re-think and re-work of every aspect of the organisation's business – carried out by the organisation itself – to create a fundamental shift in orientation and focus, towards empowerment, in every way and at every level within the enterprise.

As a result of that reorientation, the enterprise as a whole becomes more flexible, proactive, resilient, adaptable – essential attributes for any business involved in a fast-changing market. Despite the fundamental changes in approach and attitude that this demands, the process is less disruptive than it sounds – certainly less so than a typical attempt at downsizing or restructuring. As usual, all that stands in the way of those new advantages is the destructive set of habits that underlie 'business as usual' – and corporate fear, which helps no-one, especially the organisations themselves.

In that sense, the tools and concepts on the 'learning organisation', as developed by Sengé and his colleagues at MIT Sloan School of Management, are exactly complementary to what we've seen here. Their three books – *The Fifth Discipline*, *The Fifth Discipline Fieldbook* and *The Dance of Change* – provide theory, techniques, examples and case-studies in a wide range of business types. But on their own they don't address directly the basic issues of power-over and power-under which cause so many problems in any practical business context. Placed together, and used in parallel, the two sets of tools provide what is probably the most powerful and productive means available to support corporate knowledge and create qualitative organisational change.

As that first book-title suggests, Sengé's approach emphasises five distinct yet complementary disciplines:

- *systems thinking* is about holistic analysis, always looking wider than the scope of a single system: the key example used is the 'Beer Game', which demonstrates how the apparently independent actions of a brewery, its distributors and its retailers can interact in ways which seem inexplicable without a system-wide overview.
- *mental models* provide a means to 'reframe' the perception of an issue, to gain leverage towards practical solutions.
- *team learning* is a discipline in which results in the intelligence of the team being greater than that of any individual – as in the Open Source concept that "given enough eyeballs, all [software] bugs are shallow".
- *shared vision* is another name for the process of developing and maintaining corporate, team and personal purpose, much as we've seen earlier.

- *personal mastery* is the development of the skill and creativity upon which organisations ultimately depend – and which in turn depends on a solid understanding of power, response-ability and the human side of systems.

The disciplines of systems thinking and mental models emphasise a search for similarities – for patterns which are common to different arenas, and are 'self-similar' in that they recur at different levels within the same arena. One of the most useful of these – especially in the context of knowledge-technology – is the 'skills labyrinth', a common pattern in the development of every type of skill, which uses the classic single-path maze as a model of the various stages in the *personal* process of learning new skills.

The usual model of skills-development is linear: a steady increase in ability, with each layer of training building upon those before. That seems obvious, yet it doesn't describe the difficulties, the un-certainties, the common feeling of 'one step forward, two steps back', that are so often experienced in skills-development, and which make the development of new skills so challenging. The development of skill is also far more than mere training: it's *the education of experience*, literally 'out-leading' that experience from within the inner depths of each person.

The labyrinth provides a precise metaphor that addresses these issues, in a way which is common to every skill – and makes the learning of *any* skill an easier, less stressful experience.

The classic labyrinth pattern – found in many cultures around the world – is a maze with a single twisted path. There are no choices, in that there are no branches, no junctions – so as long as we can keep going, we will eventually get to the centre. Yet with all skills, reaching that central goal – the personal mastery of some aspect of the skill – can take a *lot* longer than we'd expect: and there are plenty of opportunities to get lost along the way...

The version I use for this has seven distinct sections, in what seem to be a linear order: survival, self, control, caring, communication, mind, meditation, mastery (see Figure 8). But that's not the order in which we experience them... We start with 'beginner's luck', where we succeed *because* we don't know what we're doing; then, if we keep going, we move straight into 'control' – the limited sort-of-mastery that can be attained through training. To go any deeper into the skill, we have to go outward, to look at 'self', our own involvement in the skill; and then go outward again, to the

long, slow, painful and often barely-productive 'survival' stage –
practice, practice, practice, often without much apparent point.

Figure 8: The skills-labyrinth

At the end of that section is the worst point of all, where many
people give up and abandon the skill. Traditionally known as 'the
dark night of the soul' – and the exact opposite of the exuberance
of 'beginner's luck' – it's often experienced the day before the
exam, or the first presentation before the board, or some other
crucial challenge. There *is* a way through that bleak stage: caring –
a commitment to the self and to the skill itself, as much as caring
in general – is the essential attribute that helps this happen. From
that moment on, the skills learned so far are never lost – although
as the model shows there are a few more twists and turns to go
before true mastery can be achieved!

The labyrinth model is fractal, or 'self-similar', in that it applies as
much to each stage of skills-development as to that for the overall
skill. It illustrates several common mistakes, such as the tendency
to cling on to the brief success of 'beginner's luck', which is what
leads to a common addiction to 'fast-fix' fads. It shows how interactions between people at different stages of a skill will contribute
to confusions and mistakes; for managers, it also helps explain
why productivity and proficiency will *necessarily* go down during
some stages of development. And by showing that the 'dark night
of the soul' is an inherent part of the process, it helps to reduce the
risk that people will abandon their development of skill at the
moment before success – at what would be great cost to the enterprise, and to themselves.

The core of the 'learning organisation' concept is that the learning
concerns more than just the individual and the organisation: the

development of awareness, skill and creativity must also involve the wider scope of stakeholders, because those other stakeholders are part of the overall system in which the enterprise operates. At present, few organisations do much, if anything, to foster that skill and creativity: many purport to do so – as in "our people are our greatest asset!" – but most still crush it through clumsy handling of the human side of systems. Sengé's five disciplines, combined with a better understanding of power and response-ability, presents a view of the organisation's overall activity as an integration of work, play, relate and learn – and thus provides a functional means to move out of the impasse.

This approach to organisational development also requires an end to the misleading metaphor of business as war, because it becomes obvious that assumptions about win/lose result only in destructive relationships in which *everyone* loses. The nature of business implies that competition will always be necessary: but we serve ourselves best by viewing it as competition-with, not competition-against – treating our stakeholders and competitors as *allies* in our purpose, in a greater quest for knowledge and experience.

In learning new skills, new competencies, we each face our greatest 'enemy': ourselves. We learn to face fears of inadequacy, uncertainty, powerlessness, and much else. We face that weird moment of insanity when "I can't" coincides with "I can". No-one else forces us to do this: in facing these aspects of expanding our own skills and knowledge, there's no-one else to compete against, so we can only compete with ourselves – with the help, and the power-with, of others. There's no point in playing win/lose: there's no-one to 'win' *from*, and only one possible 'loser'...

And slowly – if sometimes too slowly – the realisation dawns that the same applies in other contexts too. 'I' and 'We' interweave; it becomes obvious that 'Them' are also part of 'Us', and thus *are* 'Us' and 'We' and 'I'. At that point, our purpose, our relationships and our knowledge all combine in truly powerful ways – and powerful for everyone involved. If we want our organisations to be productive – and profitable – it's the only way to go.

PUTTING IT INTO PRACTICE

...or, "What do we do on Monday morning?"

First things first: slow down! It's usual, after reading something like this, to want to rush in and make changes straight away: but in this case, as in so many others, doing so would be likely only to make things worse. The power-problems in business and elsewhere usually arise from very deep roots: trying to 'fix' them at the surface level may create short-term surface changes, but unless the issues *are* tackled right down at the roots, the problems just reappear elsewhere, or in a different form. And the only way to reach those roots is to slow down: as the old joke puts it, "don't just do something: stand there!"

More specifically, what's most needed is 'non-ado', or 'doing no-thing' – to use the classic Taoist term for this process. It's not 'doing for the sake of doing', but it's not doing nothing, either. What we do is provide a focus for the 'doing no-thing', which in this case is those definitions I've used in the main introduction: about power and response-ability, about power-over and power-under, about subject- and object-based attitudes, about ownership, stewardship, possession and the rest. To make this easier, I've collated all these definitions into an extra section, as *Appendix: Definitions and diagnostics*. Read them again; write them somewhere easily accessible, or better still commit them to memory.

Using those definitions and questions as a focus, watch what's going on around you. Watch all the 'power-transactions' at work, at home, on the streets, on the television, anywhere; watch in particular your *own* involvement in those transactions. Note all the confusions about power: note how 'authority without account-ability' in any of its myriad forms is so often mistaken for real power, 'the ability to work / play / learn / relate'. Notice how the 'play' element of the work/play/learn triad – and even the 'learn' element – will so often be suppressed in favour of 'work / work / work'; note the real loss of functional power that occurs whenever such suppression takes place. Notice the loss of power wherever work, play, learn and relate are out of balance – too much 'play' as well as too much 'work'. Notice the ways in which people get 'taken over' by the Mask of a role – manager, salesman, teacher, parent – and remember that taking on such 'outside' habits as one's own will result in loss of personal choice, and hence loss of personal power.

Notice the prevalence of win/lose as a transaction strategy; and remember that win/lose is actually an illusory form of lose/lose. Notice the prevalence of object-based and subject-based attitudes, where people treat others as objects, or as subjects that they're 'entitled' to punish if those others act other than in accordance with expectations; and remember the self-centredness and lack of maturity that underlie those common behaviours. Notice the prevalence of power-over and power-under as a marketing strategy – perhaps by trying to create a feeling of inadequacy which could only be 'resolved' by buying the product: notice how you *feel* in response to that kind of message. Notice the prevalence of the belief that we can prop ourselves up by putting others down, that feelings of powerlessness can be permanently exported to others. Notice the prevalence of the belief that power is the ability to *avoid* work, that personal responsibility can be permanently exported to others; and remember that in every such incident, there's a loss of real power – in which *everyone* loses as a result.

Notice how power-over, power-under and the like are almost the norm rather than the exception: everywhere around us, people are trying to 'take' power from everyone else – even though it never actually works. Yet notice, too, how in this midst of all this chaos, some work *does* get done – and likewise play, and relate, and learn – which means that real power does always occur, despite all the distortions. Notice how and where that power arises, in others, and from within yourself. Notice how it's created with others, *between* yourself and others, in cooperation-with and competition-with; and notice how it gets lost in cooperation-against, and competition-against.

Observe all of this, as it happens, all around you, with you, and through you.

For *at least a week*, do nothing else: just watch. Perhaps write a few notes to yourself about what you see; perhaps tell a few others about what you're doing, and why; but do nothing more than that. And notice how hard it is to *not* try to change what you see...

Thereafter, keep observing, but also notice any opportunities that present themselves for you to change power-over or power-under into productive power-with. When such opportunities arise, take what action you can, to change your own behaviour and responses to those incidents. Put the theory into practice – though note that it's *practice*, so you're likely to make a fair few 'mis-takes' at first. Don't worry about this – in all of history, no-one's ever got it right all the time, and you're not likely to be the first! Just do what you can – and notice what happens as you do so.

Remember, too, that you're responsible for the behaviour of only one person: *you*. No-one else but you. We each can, and generally should, be responsible *about* others, and *to* others – that's power-with, in fact – yet we can never be responsible *for* others and their behaviour. That distinction is subtle, but utterly crucial. We can never change others directly: the most we can do is change *ourselves*, and provide conditions under which others may choose to change to follow suit. Above all, *don't* use this watching as a new means to criticise or control others: that would itself be power-over or power-under, which would only make things worse! If in doubt, there's a simple test: if you don't find it *personally* challenging, at least in part, then it may just be another attempt at export on your part...

All those confusions ultimately arise from a single mistake: the idea that personal issues – personal feelings and personal fears – can be 'exported' to others. This mistake is reinforced by habit: feeling leads automatically to response, without any kind of gap between. So the purpose of all this 'doing no-thing' is create and expand that gap, providing a space for reflection, for choice – and for power. "I am not that which changes: I am that which *chooses*": by creating choice, we then have power to share.

When you've had some practice at observing and addressing these power-issues, turn your attention to the enterprise as a whole. Does the enterprise have a defined purpose? If it does, to what extent – if any – do the actions in the enterprise reflect that nominal purpose? Does the purpose include all potential stakeholders – or only a few selected groups, such as customers and shareholders? To what extent do you find yourself in alignment with that purpose? To what extent do the organisation's structures and other 'internal' relationships promote functional power – as opposed to power-over and power-under? To what extent are the marketing strategies and other relations with 'outside' stakeholders based on functional power, rather than power-over or power-under? What is the balance of work, relate, learn and play – and hence of purpose-fulfilment, relationship management and knowledge-technology, and their integration – within each area of the enterprise? Explore some of those questions in the same way as you've done with the power-issues: observe carefully, then 'do no-thing' wherever you can about what you see.

> You may also find the SEMPER diagnostic and metric useful for this stage. For more details, see the chapters on SEMPER in the book *SEMPER and SCORE: enhancing enterprise effectiveness*, or the website www.sempermetrics.com .

Once you've reached this point, it'll be the right time to dip into the 'toolkit' of ideas on systems thinking, on power and response-ability, and on new views of business-relationships and business-purpose. If I had to pick just four books, they'd be the following:

- Eric Raymond's *The Cathedral and the Bazaar* (www.tuxedo.org/~esr/writings/cathedral-bazaar/), on the principles of the Open Source movement, which also provide guidelines on how to operate in a climate in which it's organisations, not employees, who have to earn the loyalty of others;
- The *Cluetrain Manifesto* (www.cluetrain.com), on the impact of the Internet on business, and the need to encourage stakeholders to become more involved in the organisation's work;
- Stephen Covey's *Principle-Centred Leadership* (www.franklincovey.com), extending his 'Seven Habits' personal-development model into the management arena;
- Peter Sengé's *The Fifth Discipline* (www.fieldbook.com), which describes the five key disciplines – systems thinking, mental models, personal mastery, shared vision and team learning – which underpin the adaptable 'learning organisation'.

The last of these is the only one which is fairly heavy going – though you're likely to find it easier, having read this, than if going into it cold. Its more practice-oriented sequels – *The Fifth Discipline Fieldbook* and *The Dance of Change* – would also be my choice for the next two 'essential reading' items.

So – over to you. Enjoy!

APPENDIX: DEFINITIONS AND DIAGNOSTICS

Definitions

Power is the ability to work/play/learn/relate, as an expression of personal choice, personal responsibility and personal purpose.

Power-from-within is the ability to source and access human power from within the self.

Power-with is the ability to assist each other to generate and access power-from-within, and to share that power with others.

Power-over is any attempt, in any form whatsoever, to create the illusion of empowering the self by disempowering any other.

Power-under is any attempt to offload responsibility onto another, or to take responsibility from another, without their express involvement and consent.

Response-ability is the ability to choose and act upon appropriate responses to events, in relation to personal purpose and shared purpose.

The **spiritual dimension of work** is the personal experience of meaning, purpose and belonging – a sense of self and of relationship with that which is greater than self, within and through the process of work itself.

An **object-based attitude** is one in which the Other is regarded as an inanimate object entirely separate from self.

A **subject-based attitude** is one in which the Other is regarded as a subject which exists only as a subordinate extension of self.

Control is an operational approach in which processes are rendered predictable through the application of defined rules to the relevant factors of the process.

Direction is an operational approach in which outcomes of processes are rendered manageable through measurement of feedback within the process in relation to a defined overall aim or purpose.

Economy is the management of the household, in a manner which is effective, reliable, elegant and appropriate to the respective context and scale.

Possession (dysfunctional ownership) is an assertion of exclusive right to exploit a resource, without reference or responsibility to others, either in the present or elsewhen.

Stewardship (functional ownership) is an assertion of responsibility for the appropriate management of the exploitation of a resource.

A **generic purpose-statement**: To improve the economic well-being and quality of life of all stakeholders.

Property

Any 'property' or asset is an intersection of four distinct categories or dimensions of reality, summarised as follows:

Physical *(behavioural)*

- *Existence*: tangible
- *Source relative to self*: external
- *Assign to others*: yes ('alienable')
- *Common property*: 'the Commons'

Mental *(conceptual)*

- *Existence*: virtual, expressed as object or action
- *Source relative to self*: internal? external? both? neither?
- *Assign to others*: expression only ('non-alienable')
- *Common property*: 'the Public Domain'

Emotional *(relational)*

- *Existence*: virtual, expressed in behaviours
- *Source relative to self*: shared between two or more parties
- *Assign to others*: difficult to transfer; assignment is legally dubious, yet common purported (e.g. as 'goodwill')
- *Common property*: none?

Spiritual *(aspirational)*

- *Existence*: virtual, expressed in behaviours

- *Source relative to self*: internal, relationship with self, also one-way 'relationship' to Other ('belonging')
- *Assign to others*: cannot be transferred; assignment is legally dubious, yet often purported (e.g. as valuation of morale)
- *Common property*: none?

An asset will often emphasise just one or two of these dimensions (for example, an object: Physical; a book: Physical + Mental), but in principle all dimensions will and must be present.

Integration of these dimensions of property is fundamental to the sustainability and/or self-regeneration of the property.

Either consciously, or unconsciously via individual unawareness or a culture's assumptions, the integration of a property may be split, resulting in undesirable 'anti-property' being assigned to others, either in the present or elsewhen.

- As defined above, possession is an ownership-model based on asserted and/or arbitrarily-assigned 'rights'
- Anti-possession is the implicit or enforced assignment to others of anti-property
- As defined above, stewardship is an ownership-model based on asserted and explicitly-accepted responsibilities
- Long-term sustainability is possible only under a stewardship model of ownership
- In terms of the power-definitions above, 'rights' without responsibilities are inherent abuse (power-under)

A power/property-diagnostic

The diagnostic consists of a suite of questions which invite interpretation of a given context, by assessment of the conditions of the context in the light of these definitions.

Use the questions here as a checklist to explore power-issues and property-issues in any context. In particular, note any split-off of anti-property, and the dysfunctional forms of power (power-over or power-under) used to create and maintain the split: basing any part of a business-model on split-off of anti-property (such as waste, pollution, creation of social stress and suchlike) will render the entire business-model fragile and unsustainable in the longer term.

128

Power

The aim of these questions is to explore ways to support the purpose, and minimise power-problems that could distract from the purpose.

- What is the overall purpose in the context? (for each individual, and for each of the collective levels)
- What are the choices in the context? Who has the 'response-ability' for those choices? To what extent does the activity represent an "expression of personal choice, personal responsibility and personal purpose" by each individual? (rather than imposed through attempted power-over and/or power-under)
- What work is to be done, and in what form? What energies, and hence form or forms of power-from-within, are required within the activity? (physical, emotional, mental, spiritual)
- Who already has the required energies available from within themselves, and/or can assist in their arising from within others? (power-from-within, power-with)
- What support is provided structurally for the required energies? (within the group, organisation, culture, society, etc; also the absence of such structural support, such as in culturally-created or -condoned power-against)
- Are any stakeholders treated as Other? What safeguards - if any – exist to ensure that *all* stakeholders are included within an overall 'win/win'? (includes non-human or non-immediate stakeholders - the environment, for example, or past or future societies)
- Is there any tendency to attempt to resolve power-issues through disempowering any Other or self, either in the present or elsewhen? (power-over) If so, what forms do such attempts take? What action - if any - could be taken to minimise such tendencies?
- Is there any tendency to attempt to resolve power-issues through transferring responsibility to or from any Other, either in the present or elsewhen? (power-under) If so, what forms do such attempts take? What action - if any - could be taken to minimise such tendencies?
- Is there any tendency to describe power-over or power-under *as* 'power'? If so, what safeguards - if any - are in place to redress this tendency?

- If the activity includes competition or cooperation, is it ultimately 'with' or 'against'? What safeguards - if any - are in place to ensure that such is 'with' rather than 'against'?

Property

The aim of these questions is to explore the nature of the property, and ensure that it is appropriately managed within and beyond its immediate context.

- What are the attributes / dimensions of the property? (Ask "What *is* the property?" before asking "Who has it?") Are these dimensions appropriately identified in the management of the property?
- What are the responsibilities for the property? Who holds / accepts / avoids them? What is the mix of possession and stewardship in the ownership-model for the property?
- Is the property integrated, in place/time? Is there any split into anti-property? If the property is split, to which Other(s) is the anti-possession assigned?

Power and property

The aim of these questions is to explore ways to support the sustainability of the property in relation to the required purpose.

- What power is needed in relation to this property? For what purpose?
- What power would be needed in order to support sustainability and/or self-regeneration of the property?
- If anti-property is split off from the property, to what extent is the split conscious / intentional or unconscious / unaware? At what layers and in what contexts does the split occur?
- If anti-possession is assigned, what power-structures create and maintain that assignment? What forms of power-against are used within those structures to maintain the split and prevent re-integration of responsibilities ('the return of the scapegoat')?

www.ingramcontent.com/pod-product-compliance
Lightning Source LLC
Chambersburg PA
CBHW021601210326
41599CB00010B/545